REAL CHRISTIANITY

A PRACTICAL VIEW OF THE PREVAILING RELIGIOUS SYSTEM OF PROFESSED CHRISTIANS IN THE HIGHER AND MIDDLE CLASSES OF THIS COUNTRY CONTRASTED WITH REAL CHRISTIANITY

William Wilberforce

Edited by
DR VINCENT EDMUNDS

HODDER AND STOUGHTON
LONDON   SYDNEY   AUCKLAND   TORONTO

British Library Cataloguing in Publication Data

Wilberforce, William
  Real Christianity
  1. Christianity
  I. Title   II. Edmunds, Vincent
  200

  ISBN 0-340-50291-6

Contents

Search the Scriptures
(John 5:39)

Not harsh and crabbed, as dull fools suppose,
But musical as is Apollo's lute.
And a perpetual feast of nectar'd sweets,
Where no crude surfeit reigns.
(John Milton *Comus*)

EDITOR'S INTRODUCTION

The name of Wilberforce is closely linked in history with the prolonged and eventually successful campaign to abolish the slave-trade. It was a long and often disappointing campaign, which brought him a considerable amount of disapproval, especially from the cities like Liverpool, whose prosperity at the time was very dependent financially on the trade. Much of the opposition came from the peerage and the early Bills aimed at limiting the trade were thrown out by the House of Lords. However, history does not always record in such detail the deep Christian faith which inspired and sustained Wilberforce in the pursuit of his avowed aim to get rid of the slave-trade. Shortly after his conversion he commented, 'God Almighty has put before me two great objects – the abolition of the slave-trade and the reformation of the manners of England.'

Born in 1759, William Wilberforce was the son of a wealthy Yorkshire merchant. Happily, this financial situation continued, so that he never had any concerns over money, though he was always more than generous in sharing it and giving it away, sometimes to undeserving causes. His home does not appear to have been particularly Christian, though he had an aunt in Wimbledon who had come under the influence of Wesley and Whitfield. The young Wilberforce was staying with her at the time, while attending school. It is not possible to estimate what effect this had on the young lad at that stage because as soon as his mother heard of the aunt's conversion he was taken back home to Hull and sent to the local grammar school. One of the ushers there, however – Isaac Milner – was a deeply religious man who was to have a considerable influence on

Wilberforce. He subsequently became in turn Vice-Chancellor of Cambridge University and then, in 1791, Dean of Carlisle.

Wilberforce was a small, rather frail man. He had a stoop which was attributed to his short-sightedness. He was, however, gifted with a great brain and a cheerful outgoing personality. He was an excellent conversationalist and much in demand with society hostesses in consequence, formidable though gracious in debate, with a great sense of humour and a good singing voice. His arrival at social functions was always greeted with approval.

At the early age of 21 Wilberforce was elected MP for Hull and remained so for the next forty-five years. William Pitt, who subsequently became the youngest prime minister, was an exact contemporary with Wilberforce at Cambridge, though their deep and lasting friendship only really blossomed after Wilberforce entered Parliament. They spent many hours together, often late into the night in conversation and discussion.

It was in 1784 that Wilberforce happened to meet Milner again and he invited him to join in a trip to the South of France that he was about to make. On the journey they read and discussed Doddridge's *Rise and Progress of Religion*. This seems to have been the start of a change in Wilberforce's outlook and thinking. There was a further trip with Milner when they read the New Testament in Greek together. A long period of depression followed as Wilberforce became increasingly aware of his own sinfulness, eventually ending in a visit to see John Newton, vicar of St Mary Woolnoth. This one-time captain of a slave ship, but now on fire for Christ, was able to comfort Wilberforce, and gradually he seems to have arrived at a state of peace and tranquillity as he received the assurance of God's forgiveness. It was not without some apprehension that he shared the subject of his new-found faith with Pitt who, though not himself a believer, still continued to respect and to rely on the advice, support and judgment of his old friend.

At this time, Wilberforce's way of life changed, for while

still in great demand in society and still an amiable guest, he had little stomach for many of its activities. Now when not forced by duties to live in Westminster, he stayed in rooms in a house in Clapham. There he was surrounded by a small circle of like-minded Christians who were nicknamed 'The Clapham Sect'. The group included Granville Sharp, Charles Grant, John Shore, William Smith, James Stephen, Edmond Eliot, John Venn, Harry Thornton and Zachary Macaulay. All but Macaulay and Venn served in one or other of the Houses of Parliament. Venn was the minister at the local church in Clapham, where they all worshipped. In addition, there were others who were frequent visitors, including among them Milner, along with the wives and some children of the regular members. They shared a common concern for the declining standards of morality in the country at that time and saw the need for a return by its people to true religion.

It was in April 1797 that Wilberforce published what was to be his major work. Its full title was *A Practical View of the Prevailing Religious System of Professed Christians in the Higher and Middle Classes of this Country contrasted with Real Christianity*. He started to write it in 1793, after many months of thought and study. Time in the House, preoccupation with the slave-trade and the war in France meant that he could snatch only an hour here and there in which to write a page or two. Over four years the book gradually took shape and was eventually five hundred pages long. Concern was expressed by well-wishers that the publication by Wilberforce of what was regarded as a religious tract could do his political career no good at all. Furthermore, his publisher was very reluctant to take the manuscript, agreeing to do so only when he was assured that Wilberforce's name would appear on the cover as the author. He then took the risk and, with considerable misgivings, printed five hundred copies. It was an instant success. All copies were sold within a few days and by August of that year five editions and 7,500 copies had been printed. By 1837 one more edition and fifteen impressions had appeared in England and twenty-six in America. It had also been translated into French, German, Italian, Spanish and Dutch.

Paul's letter to the Romans has been referred to by some as the fifth Gospel. It is certainly his own special and inspired account of man's desperate plight, apart from God, and of his justification by faith in Jesus Christ. In the same way this major work by Wilberforce could, in a sense, be called his Gospel. He is deeply aware, throughout the book, of man's hopeless, lost condition deserving only the judgment of God. He gives constant reminders of God's holiness and righteousness. These themes are reiterated as he addresses himself to the nominal Christianity of his day. His knowledge and use of Scripture is impressive and in many places direct quotations, usually without references, are woven into the fabric of his sentences.

This present book is an attempt to introduce Wilberforce's thinking to a twentieth-century readership. Most of the themes with which he deals are timeless and very relevant to our own spirituality. It is taken from the edition published in 1885 by John Davis. It admits on the title page that 'the language in some places is slightly condensed and a few passages have been omitted which appeared to be irrelevant to the present times.' However, it can be recommended to any reader who wishes to get closer to the original. A similar line has been adopted here in that the language, where obscure, circuitous or repetitive, has been updated without, it is hoped, changing the sense or thrust of the argument. This alone has led to a considerable shortening of the book. There are also some paragraphs (whole or in part) in the original, where allusions or illustrations were clearly topical but are no longer relevant. These have been omitted, without, we believe, weakening or detracting from Wilberforce's thesis.

Near the end of his book he writes:

Let the prayers of the Christian reader be also offered up for the success of this feeble endeavour in the service of true religion. God can give effect to the weakest effort; and the writer will feel himself too much honoured, if by that which he has now been making, but a single fellow-creature should be awakened from a false security, or a single Christian who deserves the name, be animated to more extensive usefulness [sic].

What better request could we also make, or hope to express, to the reader of this small volume?

V. Edmunds

INTRODUCTION
(from the 1885 edition)

The writer's main object is not to convince the sceptic, or to answer the arguments of those who oppose Christian doctrines, but to point out the scanty and erroneous system of most of those classed as orthodox Christians, and to contrast their defective scheme with what the author understands to be real Christianity. He has often observed with deep concern that such people have scant knowledge of the real nature and principles of their religion. The subject is of infinite importance; do not let it be driven out of our minds by the rush of life and the empty pleasures. Soon this present scene, with all its cares and gaieties, will be rolled away, and 'we will all stand before God's judgment seat' (Rom. 14:10). This awful consideration prompts the writer to express himself with greater freedom and justifiable frankness, and will, he trusts, secure him a serious and patient reading.

If what is stated appears needlessly austere and rigid, the writer would ask not to be condemned, without a fair examination as to whether or not his statements accord with Scripture. To that test he refers with confidence; and it must be conceded by those who accept its authority that there can be no appeal against the decision of the word of God.

I

INADEQUATE CONCEPTIONS OF THE IMPORTANCE OF CHRISTIANITY

Popular notions – Scripture account – Ignorance in this case criminal – Two false maxims exposed us

It has to be admitted that most professing Christians have a very inadequate concept of the importance of Christianity in general, of its peculiar nature and superior excellence. Listening to their conversation, virtue is praised and vice is censured; godliness perhaps is applauded and evil condemned. So far so good, but examine these meaningless generalities more closely and you will find that homage is paid not to Christianity in particular, but at best to religion in general or even to mere morality. With Christianity they are little acquainted; their views of it have been so cursory and superficial, that far from discerning its characteristic essence, they have little more than perceived those external facts which distinguish it from other forms of religion. They know some few facts, and perhaps some leading doctrines and principles, but of the consequences, relations and practical uses of these, they have few or no ideas.

When their way of life and conduct are looked at, is it possible to discern any difference between them and professed unbelievers? In an age when unbelief abounds, do we observe in them any concern to instruct their children in the principles of their faith and to furnish them with arguments for its defence? They would blush if their children were ignorant of worldly things or social graces and accordingly these are cultivated with assiduity. But the study of Christianity has formed no part of their education,

13

and their attachment to it, where there is any, is merely the result of being born in a Christian country. When this is the hereditary religion handed down from generation to generation, it is not surprising to observe young men shaken by frivolous objections and unworthy arguments. One would not expect that those who show so little attention to this aspect of their children's education would be any more observant in other areas of conduct. For here they lack the stimulus derived from affection and a sense of responsibility. In consequence they show little regard for the state of Christianity in their own country, and are indifferent about communicating the truth to those who 'sit in darkness' (Isa. 42:7).

But it may be argued that religion is not noisy and ostentatious; it is modest and private and resides within the individual. Be it so.

Now if we eavesdrop on their private conversation, we may then discover the true principles of their rights and wrongs – the scale by which they measure life's good and evil. Here, however, you will discover few or no traces of Christianity, which scarcely finds a place amid the many objects of their hopes and fears, and joys and sorrows. They may rightly be grateful for health, talents, affluence and other blessings. But they scarcely number among these the bounty of God's providence. If mentioned at all, it is noticed coldly and formally, like some obsolete claim to which, though but of small account in the estimate of our wealth or power, we think it as well to make reference in deference to the family or national habit.

When their conversation is more serious, then here surely their religion, modest and retiring as it is, must become apparent? But no, you will look in vain for the religion of Jesus. Their standard of right and wrong is not that of the Gospel. They have a different rule, advancing principles and maintaining opinions altogether opposite to the genius and characters of Christianity.

The truth is, their opinions are not formed from the study of the word of God. The Bible lies unopened, while they would be wholly ignorant of its contents, except for what

14

they hear occasionally in church, or for some faint memories retained from childhood.

How different, and in many respects contradictory, are these moral systems. One is formed from the commonly received maxims of the Christian world, while the other derives from the study of holy Scriptures!

How criminal this voluntary ignorance must appear in the sight of God! All who believe that we are creatures accountable to God (and only to such is the writer addressing himself) will admit that one day we shall have to answer to the Almighty for all the means and opportunities we have enjoyed of improving ourselves, or of promoting the happiness of others. And if we shall be called upon to answer for the use made of our bodily organs, and of the means of relieving the wants and necessities of our fellow-creatures, how much more shall we have to give account for the exercise of the nobler and more exalted faculties of our nature – invention, judgment, memory, diligent application, serious reflection and honest decision! When God has of His goodness granted us such an abundant means of instruction in that which concerns our eternal interests, how great must be the guilt, and how awful the punishment of voluntary ignorance!

And why should we in this single pursuit expect knowledge without enquiry, and success without endeavour? Nature teaches us a different lesson, which is confirmed by our experience. The bountiful gifts of Providence are not so bestowed as to give rise to indolence, but rather to rouse us to action. No one expects to attain to the height of learning arts, power, or wealth, without vigorous resolution, strenuous diligence, and steady perseverance. Yet we expect to be Christians without labour, study, or enquiry. This is the more preposterous, since Christianity is a revelation from God, and not the invention of man. It reveals to us new relations with their corresponding duties; it contains doctrines, motives, practical principles and rules peculiar to itself. These are almost as new in their nature as they are supreme in their excellence. We cannot reasonably expect to become proficient in its practice by the accidental experiences of life, as one might learn insensibly the maxims of worldly policy, or a scheme of mere morals.

The diligent perusal of Scripture uncovers our past ignorance. We should not let ourselves be deceived by outward appearances, or let the philosophical theory confound the Gospel of Christ. Rather we should allow the truth so much forgotten, and which cannot be too strongly insisted on, that Christianity calls on us, not merely in general to be religious and moral, but specially to believe the doctrines, imbibe the principles and practise the precepts of Christ. Christianity is always represented in Scripture as the grand, unparalleled instance of God's bounty to mankind. It was graciously held forth in the original promise to our first parents. It was predicted by a long continued series of prophets and was the subject of their prayers, inquiries, and longing expectations. In a world which opposed and persecuted them, it was their source of peace, hope and consolation. At last it approached – the desire of all nations – a host of angels hailed its introduction and proclaimed its character, 'Glory to God in the highest, and on earth peace to men on whom his favour rests' (Luke 2:14). It is represented figuratively in Scripture in such a way as most deeply to impress on us its value. It is spoken of as light from darkness, as release from prison, as deliverance from captivity, as life from death. 'Sovereign Lord, as you have promised, you now dismiss your servant in peace. For my eyes have seen your salvation' (Luke 2:29–30) was the exclamation with which it was welcomed by the pious Simeon. The Good News was universally received and professed among the early converts with thankfulness and joy. At one time, its communication is promised as a reward; at another, the loss of it is threatened as a punishment. And, short as is the Lord's Prayer, the more general extension of the kingdom of Christ constitutes one of its leading petitions.

What exalted conceptions of the importance of Christianity should fill our hearts as we read these descriptions! Yet, in vain have we 'precept upon precept; line upon line' (Isa. 28:10 AV). The Good News was predicted, prayed and longed for, announced, characterised and rejoiced in, yet we scarcely accept this heavenly treasure poured into our lap in rich abundance! We turn from it coldly, or at best handle it negligently, like something of little value. But a proper sense of its value would most certainly be impressed on us by the diligent study of God's word, that mine of divine truth and consolation. It is here that we learn our obligations and duties, our faith and practice. Surely it should not be necessary to press men to peruse the sacred volume. Reason dictates, revelation commands; 'faith comes from hearing the message, and the message is heard through the word of Christ' (Rom. 10:17). 'You diligently study the Scriptures' (John 5:39). 'Always be prepared to give an answer to everyone who asks you to give the reason for the hope that you have' (1 Pet. 3:15). Such are the declarations and injunctions of the inspired writers; those who obey these injunctions, witness to their value in their lives. Yet, sadly, with the Bible in our homes, we are ignorant of its contents. Small wonder that the bulk of the Christian world knows so little, and errs so greatly, concerning the religion which they profess.

This is not the place for a full enquiry as to why those who hold that the Bible is the word of God, and who profess to rest their hopes on the Christian basis, are content to remain in a state of such lamentable ignorance. There are, however, two kindred opinions, from which this state of affairs appears to derive much support. The one is what a man believes is of little importance, rather look at his behaviour. The other is that sincerity is all that matters. Let a man's opinions and conduct be what they may, provided he is sincerely convinced that they are right, then in the sight of God he cannot be a wrong-doer!

It would detain us too long to set forth the various merits of these favourite positions. The former is founded on that grossly fallacious assumption that a man's opinions will not influence his practice. The latter proceeds on this ground-less supposition that God has not afforded us sufficient means for discriminating between truth and falsehood,

17

right and wrong. It implies that however wild and extravagant a man's opinions or conduct, they are nevertheless as much the result of impartial enquiry and honest conviction as if his sentiments and actions had been strictly conformable to the rules of reason and sobriety. Never, indeed, was there a principle more general in its use, more sovereign in its potency. It can be argued that however heinous a crime our individual has committed, if it was felt sincerely to be the right thing to do, then that person is innocent of the crime! This principle might be shown to be even more absurd than has been stated. It would not be going too far to assert, that while it scorns to defend petty villains who still retain the sense of good and evil, it holds forth a secure asylum to those more hardened criminals who from repeated crimes are lost alike to the perception as the practice of virtue. It selects a seared conscience, and a heart become callous to all moral distinctions, as the special objects of its care. Not only in criminal history are instances like these° to be found, of persons committing the greatest crimes with a sincere conviction of the rightness of their conduct. Scripture affords us parallels, and surely it was to guard us against this very error that the Lord forewarned His disciples, 'a time is coming when anyone who kills you will think he is offering a service to God' (John 16:2).

A principle like this must then be abandoned and those who advocate sincerity must be made to see that it must also imply honesty of mind, the faithful use of the means of knowledge and of improvement, the desire to be instructed, humble enquiry, impartial consideration and unprejudiced judgment. It is to these attitudes of mind that we should earnestly call you, always praying fervently for God's blessing. Scripture contains many encouraging promises relevant to this. 'Ask, and it will be given to you; seek, and you will find; knock, and the door will be opened to you' (Luke 11:9).

'Come, all you who are thirsty, come to the waters' (Isa. 55:1). Such are the comfortable assurances, such the gracious encouragements to the truly sincere enquirer. How great will be our guilt if we slight these merciful offers!

How many prophets and kings have desired to hear the things that we hear, and have not heard them! Great indeed are our opportunities; great also is our responsibility. Let us be aware of our position. We have every reason to arouse our fears, or to stimulate our industry. Only too soon our days may be ended. Or, should our long-suffering God continue to give us the mercies which we so much abuse, this will only aggravate our crime and in the end enhance our guilt. The time of reckoning will come at last. And when finally summoned to the bar of God, to give an account of our stewardship, what plea can we have to urge in our defence, if we remain willingly and obstinately ignorant of the way which leads to life, with such transcendent means of knowing it and such urgent motives to pursue it?

II

CORRUPTION OF HUMAN NATURE

Section 1
Inadequate conceptions of the corruption of human nature

After considering the defective ideas of the importance of Christianity in general, the first specific misconceptions which we consider concern the corruption and weakness of human nature. This subject is of the deepest importance. It lies at the very root of all true religion. It is eminently the basis, the groundwork of Christianity.

Most professed Christians either overlook altogether, deny, or greatly extenuate the corruption and weakness here in question. They acknowledge that there is, and always has been in the world, a great deal of vice and wickedness. They will admit that man has always been prone to sensuality and selfishness, contrary to the more refined and liberal principles of his nature; that in all ages and countries, in public and in private life, innumerable instances can be found of oppression, rapacity, cruelty, fraud, envy and malice. They will admit that too often in vain one informs the understanding, and convinces the judgment. They admit that you do not reform the hearts of men by this means. Knowing their duty, they will not practise it; not even when they have been forced to acknowledge that the path of virtue is also that of true interest and solid enjoyment.

These facts are certain and cannot be disputed. But though these effects of human depravity are acknowledged and regretted, they are not traced to their true origin. Rather you are told of frailty and infirmity, petty transgressions, occasional failings, of sudden lapses, and of

20

such other qualifying terms as may serve to keep out of view the true source of the evil. They do not shock the understanding, but rather console human pride. Most professed Christians regard man as naturally pure and inclined to all virtue, but sometimes, almost involuntarily, led astray, or overpowered by the violence of temptation. Vice by them is regarded as a temporary accident rather than a constitutional and habitual disorder; it is a poisonous plant living and even thriving in the human mind; it is not the natural growth and product of the soil.

Far different is the humiliating language of Christianity. We learn that man is an apostate creature, fallen from his high beginnings, degraded in his nature and depraved in his faculties. He is disposed not to good, but to evil. Vice is natural and easy to him. Virtue is difficult and laborious. He is tainted with sin, not slightly and superficially, but radically and to the very core. These are Scripture truths which, however mortifying to our pride, cannot be gainsaid. This truth comes home forcibly when we contemplate the contrast between what still remains to us of our primitive dignity, and our present state of moral degradation.

> Into what depth thou seest,
> From what height fallen.
>
> Milton, *Paradise Lost*, Book 1

Let us look first at the natural powers and faculties of man – his invention, reason, judgment and memory. He has a mind 'of large discourse', 'looking before and after', reviewing the past, determining the present and anticipating the future. He can discern, collect, combine, and compare. This mind is capable of comprehending and admiring the beauty of moral excellence. It can warn and animate fear and hope; to solace and soften joy and sorrow; attach with love, harmonise with sympathy, attempt with courage, endure with patience and with the power of conscience, that faithful monitor within the breasts, enforce reasons, conclusions, and direct and regulate the soul's passions. Truly, we must pronounce him 'majestic though in ruin.'

'Happy, happy world!' would be the exclamation of the inhabitant of some other planet on being told of a globe like ours, peopled with such creatures as these, and abounding with situations and occasions which call forth the multiplied excellences of their nature.

So much for man's natural powers. Let us now see the uses to which he applies them. Review the whole picture; view him in every age, climate, nation, every condition and period of society. Where do you discover the characters of his exalted nature? His reason is clouded; his affections perverted, and his conscience stupefied! Anger, envy, hatred, revenge, all spring up in his wretched bosom! He is a slave to the meanest of his appetites! What fatal propensities does he manifest to evil and what inaptitude to good!

Consider the state of the ancient world. Think not only of that benighted part where all lay buried in brutish ignorance and barbarism, but on the seats of civilised and polished nations, on the empires of taste, learning and philosophy. Even in these chosen regions where knowledge abounded, the moral darkness was so thick 'that it might be felt.' Behold their sottish idolatries, their absurd superstitions, their want of natural affection, their brutal excesses, their unfeeling oppression, their savage cruelty! Do not observe the illiterate and the vulgar, but rather the learned and refined. Do not form your opinions from the behaviour of the less restrained and more licentious for you will turn away with disgust and shame from the accepted and familiar habits of the decent and the upright. St Paul best states the facts, and furnishes the explanation: 'since they did not think it worth while to retain the knowledge of God, he gave them over to a depraved mind' (Rom. 1:28).

Now direct your view to the inhabitants of the New World – the American Indians. The baneful practices and contagious example of the old world had never travelled there. Surely, among these children of nature, we should expect to find those virtuous tendencies for which we have hitherto looked in vain. Alas, our search will still be fruitless! Robertson, the American historian, represented them as being a compound of pride, indolence, selfishness, cunning and cruelty. They were full of an insatiable desire for revenge, a ferocity which nothing could soften and were strangers to the most amiable sensibilities of nature. They appeared incapable of conjugal affection or parental fondness, filial reverence, or social attachments. Their state of barbarism contained many of the vices and weaknesses of civilised society. Their horrid treatment of captives taken in war, on whose bodies they feasted after putting them to death by the most cruel tortures, is so well known, that we may spare the disgusting recital. No commendable qualities relieve this gloomy picture, except fortitude, perseverance and zeal for the welfare of their little community.

The behaviour of the heathen nations you regard as indefensible, but wish rather to form your estimate of man from a view of countries which have been blessed with the light of God's revelation. We fully concede that Christianity has set the general tone of morals much higher than it was ever found in the pagan world. She has everywhere improved the character and multiplied the comforts of society, particularly to the poor and the weak, whom from the beginning she professed to take under her special patronage. Yet even in this more favoured situation we shall discover too many lamentable proofs of man's depravity, much now becomes even more apparent. For over what barriers does it not leap? Over what motives is it not now victorious? Consider well the superior light and advantages which we enjoy, and you will then appreciate our greater obligations. Consider how often our evil propensities are restrained by the controlling influence of positive laws, and by public opinion. Consider then the superior excellence of our moral code, the new principles of obedience furnished by the Gospel, and above all, the awful sanction derived from the clear pronouncements of a future state of retribution, and of that tremendous day when 'we will all stand before God's judgment seat' (Rom. 14:10).

Yet, in spite of all our knowledge, enforced and pressed home by these facts, how little have we progressed in virtue! It has been insufficient to prevent the adoption, in our days, of various ancient maxims, which clearly establish

23

the depravity of man. A few examples might help. It is still acknowledged that prosperity hardens the heart; that unlimited power is always abused, instead of being a means of bringing happiness; that habits of vice grow of themselves, while those of virtue, if obtained at all, are formed slowly and with difficulty. Those who draw the finest pictures of virtue, and seem most enamoured of her charms, are often the least under her influence, and by the merest trifles they are drawn aside from that line of conduct, which they most strongly and seriously recommend to others.

It may suffice to touch very slightly on some other arguments. One of these may be drawn from the perverse positions seen in children, which it is the business, sometimes ineffectual, of education to reform. Another may be drawn from the various deceits we are apt to practise on ourselves, with which we are all familiar. This kind of corruption has resulted in Christianity itself being too often disgraced, and turned into a source of cruelty. Amid the bitterness of persecution, every trace has disappeared of the mild and beneficent spirit of the religion of Jesus. How the taint must have worked itself into the frame, and have corrupted the works, when the most wholesome nutriment can be changed into the deadliest poison! Wishing always to argue from premises which are not only really sound, but also cannot even be questioned by those to whom this work is addressed, little has been said about the deplorable state of the heathen regarding their defective and unworthy conceptions of God. 'Yet he has not left himself without testimony: He has shown kindness by giving you rain from heaven, and crops in their seasons; he provides you with plenty of food and fills your hearts with joy' (Acts 14:17).

But to any who call themselves Christians, it is an astonishing instance of human depravity that we take so much for granted. We who enjoy the full light of revelation and to whom God has granted such clear evidences of what we need to know of His being and attributes and who profess to believe that 'in him we live and move and have our being' (Acts 17:28) owing to Him all the comforts we here enjoy, with the offer of eternal glory purchased for us

24

by the atoning blood of His own Son. 'Thanks be to God for his indescribable gift' (2 Cor. 9:15). Thus loaded with His mercies how can we still forget His authority, and be ungrateful for His benefits, slight His gracious proposals, or receive them in a cold and heartless manner?

But put the question concerning the natural depravity of man to the severest test by posing it to a watchful, diligent, self-denying Christian, and let him decide the controversy from his personal experience. Go with him into his closet, ask him his opinion of the corruption of the heart, and he will tell you that he is deeply aware of its power. That he has learned from much self-observation, and long acquaintance with the workings of his own mind. He will tell you that every day strengthens this conviction. Indeed, hourly he sees fresh reason to deplore his want of simplicity in intention, his weakness of purpose, his low views, his selfish, unworthy desires, his slowness to set about his duty, and his languor and coldness in performing it. He finds himself obliged continually to confess that he feels within himself two opposite principles, so that 'he cannot do the things that he would.'

Such is man's moral history and condition. The figures may vary, and the colour is sometimes darker, sometimes of a lighter hue, but the principles of the composition, the grand outlines, are everywhere the same. Wherever we look, we find the melancholy evidence of our depravity. In ancient or modern times, in barbarous or civilised nations, in the conduct of the world around us, within our own conscience, whether we read, hear, act, think, or feel, the same humiliating lesson is forced upon us.

How do we explain the differences in the picture of man as he was intended to be and his actual state? Will frailty, infirmity, occasional lapses, unguarded moments, or any such qualifying terms, convey an adequate idea of the nature, or cause of the disorder? How can we account for it, except by conceiving that man, since his creation, has contracted a taint. This subtle poison has been communicated throughout the race of Adam, exhibiting everywhere incontestable marks of its fatal malignancy. As a result our appetites have grown stronger, the value of our powers of reason and conscience have weakened. Sensual gratifications and illicit affections have debased our nobler powers and diverted our hearts from the discovery of God, the consideration of His perfections, willing submission to His authority and obedience to His laws. By repeated vicious acts, evil habits have resulted and we have been bound by sin's fetters. In consequence of our own folly, our understanding has grown darker, and our heart harder. At length reason has betrayed her trust, and conscience herself has aided the delusion, till, instead of deploring our miserable slavery, we have too often hugged, and even gloried in our chains.

Such is the progress of vice where it is permitted to reach full growth in the human heart. Circumstances of individuals will differ, but none is altogether free. All without exception, to a greater or less degree, bear about them more or less visible ignominious marks of their captivity.

How can these facts be accounted for on any other supposition than that of some original taint, or radical principle of corruption? All other solutions are unsatisfactory. So it appears that the corruption of human nature is proved by the same sort of reasoning as has been accepted as conclusive in establishing the existence, and ascertaining the laws of, the principle of gravitation. Newton's philosophy is not mere speculation, and therefore an uncertain though perhaps an ingenious theory, but it is the sure result of a large and actual experiment. It is deduced from incontestable facts, and proves its truth by harmonising with the various parts and explaining the various phenomena of the universe, which are otherwise jarring and inexplicable.

Revelation, however, comes in here, and sustains the fallible conjectures of our unaided reason. The Bible speaks of us as fallen creatures. In almost every page we find something calculated to abate the loftiness and silence the pretensions of man. '. . . every inclination of the heart is evil from childhood' (Gen. 8:21). 'What is man, that he could be pure, or one born of woman, that he should be righteous?' (Job 15:14). '. . . how much less man, who is vile and corrupt, who drinks up evil like water!' (Job 15:16). 'The Lord looks down from heaven on the sons of men to see if there are any who understand, any who seek God. All have turned aside, they have together become corrupt; there is no-one who does good, not even one' (Ps. 14:2–3). Who can say, 'I have kept my heart pure; I am clean and without sin?' (Prov. 20:9). 'The heart is deceitful above all things and beyond cure. Who can understand it?' (Jer. 17:9). 'Surely I was sinful at birth, sinful from the time my mother conceived me' (Ps. 51:5). 'Like the rest, we were by nature objects of wrath' (Eph. 2:3). 'What a wretched man I am! Who will rescue me from this body of death?' (Rom. 7:24). Numerous passages speak the same language, which can be illustrated and confirmed by various other considerations, such as those which represent a thorough change and renovation of our nature, as necessary to our becoming true Christians. We also observe that holy men attribute their good dispositions and affections solely to God's working in their lives.

Section II
Evil spirit – natural state of man

In addition to all that has been yet stated, God's word informs us that we have to contend not only with our own natural depravity, but with the power of darkness, the evil spirit, who rules in the hearts of the wicked, and whose dominion we learn is so general as to earn him the title 'the prince of this world'. There is no stronger proof of the difference existing between the religious system of the Bible and that of the bulk of nominal Christians than the proof that this subject affords. The existence and agency of the evil spirit, though so distinctly and repeatedly affirmed in Scripture, is regarded by many as a prejudice which it is a discredit to any man of understanding to believe. But to be consistent with ourselves, we might on the same principle, deny the reality of all other spiritual beings. What is there in

27

the doctrine which is in itself improbable, or which is not confirmed by analogy? We see, in fact, that there are wicked men, enemies to God, and malignant towards their fellow-creatures, who enjoy drawing in others to commit some evil deed. Why then should it be deemed incredible that there may be one or more spiritual intelligences of similar nature and propensity, who in like manner are permitted to tempt men to sin? Surely we may justly accuse our opponents of gross inconsistency in accepting without difficulty the existence and operation of these qualities in a material being, and yet denying them in an immaterial one. This is in direct contradiction to the authority of Scripture, which they accept as conclusive, when they cannot and will not pretend for a moment that there is anything belonging to the nature of matter, to which these qualities naturally adhere.

But this is a serious matter for all who form their opinions on the authority of the word of God. We are brought into captivity, exposed to danger, depraved and weakened within, and tempted from without. It might well fill our hearts with anxiety to reflect, that 'the day of the Lord will come,' when, 'the heavens will disappear with a roar; the elements will be destroyed by fire' (2 Pet. 3:10). When 'the dead, small and great, stand before God' (Rev. 20:12) and we shall have to give account of all our deeds. We are naturally prompted to turn over the page in order to discover the qualities and character of our judge, and the probable principles of His judgment, but this only serves to turn painful apprehension into fixed and certain terror. First, of the qualities of our judge, all nature bears witness to His irresistible power. So we read in Scripture that nothing can escape His observation, or remains hidden. Not our actions only, but our most secret thoughts are open to His view. 'You discern my going out and my lying down; you are familiar with all my ways' (Ps. 139:3). '– the Lord searches every heart and understands every motive behind the thoughts' (1 Chr. 28:9). 'He will bring to light what is hidden in darkness and will expose the motives of men's hearts' (1 Cor. 4:5).

Now listen to His likeness, and the standard of His judgment. 'For the Lord your God is a consuming fire, a jealous God' (Deut. 4:24). 'Your eyes are too pure to look on evil' (Hab. 1:13). 'The soul who sins is the one who will die' (Ezek. 18:4). 'For the wages of sin is death' (Rom. 6:23). These positive declarations are underlined by the accounts recorded in Scripture for our warning of God's terrible vengeance. His punishment of 'the angels who did not keep their positions of authority but abandoned their own home – these he has kept in darkness, bound with everlasting chains for judgment on the great Day' (Jude 6) is recorded as is the fate of Sodom and Gomorrah, the sentence issued against the idolatrous nations of Canaan, and the execution of which was assigned to the Israelites by the express command of God, at their own peril, in case of disobedience. The ruin of Babylon, and of Tyre, and of Nineveh, and of Jerusalem, prophetically denounced as the punishment of their crimes, took place in exact and terrible accord with divine prediction. These fearful matters should surely confound the fallacious confidence of any who claim that our Creator, while aware of our natural weakness, will be, of course, disposed to allow for it. Unable, indeed, to justify ourselves in the sight of God, we need not give way to such gloomy apprehensions, but rather throw ourselves hopefully on the infinite benevolence of the Almighty. It is indeed, true that with the threatenings of the word of God there are also many gracious offers of pardon, to the truly penitent. But, alas, whose conscience does not reproach him for having trifled with God's long suffering, and for poorly keeping those resolutions of amendment, which he had formed in times of recollection and remorse?

If such is our sad condition, what is to be done? Is there any hope? Is it 'only a fearful expectation of judgment and of raging fire that will consume the enemies of God' (Heb. 10:27)? Thank God we are not imprisoned inescapably. 'Return to your fortress, O prisoners of hope' (Zech. 9:12). Listen to the one whose calling is 'to bind up the broken-hearted, to proclaim freedom for the captives and release from darkness for the prisoners' (Isa. 61:1). Those who have formed a true idea of their lost and helpless state will gladly welcome such a deliverance. And this is the cause which renders it of such pressing moment not to pass cursorily over those important topics of the original and superinduced corruption and weakness of man; a discussion painful and humiliating to the pride of human nature, to which the mind lends itself with difficulty, and hearkens with a mixture of anger and disgust; but well suited to our case, and like the distasteful lessons of adversity, permanently useful in its consequences. It is here, never let it be forgotten, that our foundation must be laid; otherwise our superstructure, whatever we may think of it, will one day or other prove tottering and insecure. This is therefore no metaphysical speculation, but a practical matter.

Slight and superficial conceptions of our state of natural degradation, and of our insufficiency to recover from it of ourselves, fall in too well with our natural inconsiderateness, and produce that fatal insensibility to the divine warning to 'flee from the coming wrath' (Matt. 3:7), which we cannot but observe to prevail so generally. Because we have no appreciation of the severity of our disease and its dreadful outcome, we do not set ourselves to work in earnest to obtain the remedy. It must always be remembered that this deliverance is not forced on us, but offered to us. We are provided with every help, and must always remember that of ourselves we cannot will or do rightly. We are plainly admonished to 'work out your salvation with fear and trembling' (Phil. 2:12); to be watchful, for we are encompassed with dangers and to 'Put on the full armour of God' (Eph. 6:11).

May we be enabled to shake off that lethargy which is so apt to creep upon us! A deep, practical conviction of our natural depravity and weakness will be a great help here. This will not only rouse us from our false security, but also keep us wakeful and active to the end. Let us therefore make it our business to have this doctrine firmly grounded in our understandings and radically worked into our hearts.

With a view to the former of these objects, we should often seriously and attentively consider the firm ground on which it rests. It is made known to us plainly by the light of nature, and irresistibly enforced on us by the dictates of our unassisted understandings, to which is added the authoritative stamp of revelation to complete the proof. We must be altogether inexcusable if we still remain unconvinced by such an accumulated mass of argument.

But we must not only assent to the doctrine in our minds but also feel it strongly in our hearts. To this end, let us make our practice of remembering our natural depravity which is their primary cause, the sad instances of vice and folly of which we read, or which we see around us, or to which we feel the propensities in our own selves. Let us be vigilant and distrustful of ourselves while we look with kindness and pity on the faults and infirmities of others, whom we should learn to regard with the same tender concern that the sick show to those who are suffering from the same illness as themselves. Though this is a lesson which we are slow to learn, it is one in which study and experience, the incidents of every day and every fresh observation of the workings of our own hearts, will gradually concur to perfect us. Let it not in the end be our reproach and ruin, that we possess these abundant means of instruction in vain.

Section III
Corruption of human nature – Objection

Man finds it very difficult to swallow his pride. But forced to abandon the plea of innocence, an objector may seek to evade this on being pressed closely on this issue by saying: 'Whatever I am, I am what my Creator made me. If this plea does not establish my innocence, it must excuse or at least extenuate my guilt. Frail and weak as I am, a being of infinite justice and goodness will never try me by a rule which may be fair for creatures of a higher nature, but is altogether disproportionate to mine.'

The writer is not going to enter into the discussion of the major question of the origin of evil, or to attempt to reconcile its existence and consequent punishment with the acknowledged attributes and perfections of God. Yet, as such an objection as that which has been stated is sometimes heard from the mouths of professed Christians, it must not be passed by without a few brief comments.

Were the language in question to be addressed to us by an avowed sceptic, while it might not be very difficult to show him the futility of his reasoning, yet we should almost despair of satisfying him of the soundness of our own. By arguments we might at length silence our objector, but we could not hope to bring him round to our opinions. We should probably do better to lay fairly before him all the various arguments for the truth of our faith; arguments which have been sufficient to satisfy the wisest, the best and the ablest of men. We should afterwards, perhaps, insist on the abundant confirmation Christianity receives from its being exactly suited to man's nature and needs. We might conclude by asking him whether all this weight of evidence was to be turned simply by this one difficulty, on a subject so high and mysterious. We see such a small part of God's universal creation, and our faculties are wholly incompetent to judge the infinite schemes of His wisdom. This seems, at least in general, the best way to deal with this unbeliever's objection.

But it must be remembered that the present work is addressed to those who acknowledge the authority of Scripture. And in order to convince all such that there is a fallacy in our objector's reasoning, it will be sufficient to establish that though the word of God shows His justice and goodness, and also the natural depravity of man, yet it no less clearly affirms that this natural depravity will never be accepted as an excuse for sin, rather 'those who have done evil will rise to be condemned' (John 5:29) – 'The wicked return to the grave, all the nations that forget God' (Ps. 9:17). And it should be noted that our Saviour, though the messenger of peace and goodwill to man, has again and again repeated these awful denunciations.

Neither does Scripture permit us to suppose that our sins, or the dreadful consequences of them, are the responsibility of God. When tempted, no one should say 'God is tempting me. For God cannot be tempted by evil, nor does he tempt anyone' (Jas. 1:13). 'The Lord is . . . not wanting anyone to perish' (2 Pet. 3:9). And again, 'Do I take any pleasure in the death of the wicked? declares the Sovereign Lord. Rather, am I not pleased when they turn from their ways and live?' (Ezek. 18:23). 'For I take no pleasure in the death of anyone, declares the Sovereign Lord' (Ezek. 18:32). Indeed almost every page of God's word contains some warning or invitation to sinners. To a considerate mind, all these must unquestionably be proofs of our present position.

It has been important to draw attention to this objection because when not stated in such florid language it may frequently appear in more covert forms. This encourages doubt and unbelief and may give rise to a false sense of comfort and peace. Scripture clearly states man's natural corruption and weakness; it is directly opposed to the idea that this corruption and weakness will result in a lowering of the demands of divine justice, and in some way palliating our transgressions. Such an idea is totally against the whole scheme of redemption by Christ's atonement. But perhaps it will suffice when any such suggestions as we are condemning are entertained by a Christian, to advise him to silence them with this practical approach: Even though we are naturally depraved and weak, our temptations numerous, and our Almighty judge infinitely holy, yet his offer to penitent sinners of pardon, grace and strength are universal and unlimited.

However do not be surprised if we encounter situations which we cannot fully understand. There will be plenty of these. We have difficulties over natural things like the meanest reptile, or every herb and flower. All nature calls us to be humble. Can it then be surprising if we are at a loss when we consider not the properties of matter, or of numbers, but the counsels and ways of Him whose 'understanding has no limit' (Ps. 147:5)? 'How unsearchable his judgments, and his paths beyond tracing out!' (Rom. 11:33). In our ignorance, however, we can rest at peace on His declaration, 'Clouds and thick darkness surround him; righteousness and justice are the foundation of his throne' (Ps. 97:2). Always remember that if parts of Christianity are difficult to grasp, those things which we need most to know are both plain and obvious. The wise man will hold firmly to these truths while at the same time not contradicting the revealed truth which he cannot understand. Remember this instructive admonition: 'The secret things belong to the Lord our God, but the things revealed belong to us and to our children for ever, that we may follow all the words of this law' (Deut. 29:29).

III

CHIEF DEFECTS OF THE RELIGIOUS SYSTEM OF THE BULK OF PROFESSED CHRISTIANS, IN WHAT REGARDS OUR LORD JESUS CHRIST, AND THE HOLY SPIRIT – WITH A DISSERTATION CONCERNING THE USE OF THE PASSIONS IN RELIGION

Section I
Inadequate conceptions concerning our Saviour and the Holy Spirit

These are the leading doctrines concerning our Saviour, and the Holy Spirit, which are taught in Scriptures, and held by the Church of England.

That God loved the world so much that in His tender mercy He gave His only Son Jesus Christ for our redemption;
That our Lord willingly left the glory of the Father and was made man;
That 'He was despised and rejected by men, a man of sorrows, and familiar with suffering' (Isa. 53:3);
That 'He was pierced for our transgressions, he was crushed for our iniquities' (Isa. 53:5);
That 'the Lord has laid on him the iniquity of us all' (Isa. 53:6);
That at length He humbled Himself as far as to die on the cross for us miserable sinners; so that all who with genuine repentance and true faith should come to Him, might not perish, but have everlasting life;

That He is now at the right hand of God, interceding for His people;

That we have been 'reconciled to him [God] through the death of his Son' (Rom. 5:10) and so we may 'approach the throne of grace with confidence, so that we may receive mercy and find grace to help us in our time of need' (Heb. 4:16);

That our heavenly Father will 'give the Holy Spirit to those who ask him' (Luke 11:13);

That the Spirit of God must dwell in us; and that 'if anyone does not have the Spirit of Christ, he does not belong to Christ' (Rom. 8:9);

That under God's influence we are 'being renewed in knowledge in the image of its Creator' (Col. 3:10) and 'filled with the fruit of righteousness . . . to the glory and praise of God' (Phil. 1:11) so that we are gratified 'to share in the inheritance of the saints in the kingdom of light' (Col. 1:12);

Finally we shall be perfected after His likeness and admitted to His heavenly kingdom.

The truth of these affirmations will be taken for granted. They are to be found everywhere dispersed throughout our excellent liturgy. Would to God it could be presumed that all who assent to them also experience and discern their excellency in their minds and feel their power and experience, their transforming influence in their hearts. They are calculated to arouse in us a deep sense of humility and a horror of sin; with hope, firm faith, heavenly joy, ardent love and active unceasing gratitude!

But here, it is to be feared, will be found the major defect in the religion of most professed Christians. While at first this defect has little outward influence it gradually extinguishes the internal principle of true life and soon extends its benumbing influence to the remotest parts of the being. This defect is closely connected with that which was dealt with in the last chapter: 'It is not the healthy who need a doctor, but the sick' (Luke 5:31). Had we been aware of the load of our sins, which our own strength is quite unable to bear, and which must finally sink us into perdition, we should have rejoiced at the gracious invitation: 'Come to me, all you who are weary and burdened, and I will give you rest' (Matt. 11:28). But in those scarcely aware of their sins' weight it would be mere affectation to pretend to any marked failings as to the value and acceptableness of the proffered deliverance. This pretence is now seldom kept, and the most superficial observer, comparing the thoughts and views of the bulk of Christians with the articles still retained in their creed, and with the strong language of Scripture, must be struck by the amazing disproportion that exists.

Leaving aside the many from whose minds religion is totally excluded by the business or worthless pursuits of life, how about the more decent and upright? To what criterion shall we appeal? Are their hearts really filled with these things, and warmed by the love which they should inspire? If so then their minds are apt to stray to them unbidden, or at least to hasten back to them with eagerness, when they are free from the separation imposed by life's necessary cares and business.

'And how,' it may be perhaps replied, 'do you know that the minds of these people are occupied in this way?' Let us report our experiment. Talk to these people and lead the conversation around to the subject of religion. At best they will talk of things in generalities; there is nothing precise and definite, nothing which implies a mind used to contemplate the subject. You strive in vain to bring them to speak on a topic which one might expect to be uppermost in the heart of a redeemed sinner. But they elude all your endeavours; and if you mention it yourself, you meet a cool reception, if not unequivocal disgust. It is at best a forced and formal discussion. The excellence of our Saviour's moral precepts, the kindness, simplicity, self-denial and unblemished purity of His life, His patience and meekness, in the hour of death, are spoken of with admiration, when spoken of at all – as they have indeed extracted unwilling praise from the most militant unbelievers. But these are mentioned as abstract qualities rather than as the

37

perfections and features of our patron, benefactor and friend 'who loved me [us] and gave himself for me [us]' (Gal. 2:20), of Him who died 'for our sins and was raised to life for our justification' (Rom. 4:25), who is even now 'at the right hand of God and is also interceding for us' (Rom. 8:34). Who would think that the kindness, humanity, self-denial and patience in suffering, which we so drily commend, had been exerted towards us in acts of infinite benevolence, of which we were to derive the benefit in condescensions and labours submitted to for our sakes, in pain and ignominy endured for our deliverance?

Unitarians and Socinians who deny or explain away the special doctrines of the Gospel are permitted to feel and talk about these great truths with little emotion. But this coldness in those who profess a sincere belief in them, is insupportable. Man's greatest possible service to man must appear contemptible when compared with the unspeakable mercies of Christ, so dearly bought, so freely bestowed – a deliverance from eternal misery – the gift of a 'crown of glory that will never fade away' (1 Pet. 5:4). How would we judge such behaviour from one who had received outstanding help from a fellow human? True love is ardent and active and a cold, dormant, phlegmatic gratitude, are contradictions in terms. When these generous affections come over us, are we not keen to sing the praises of our benefactor? We are upset when anything disparaging is said about Him! We delight to tell of His kindness! We carefully preserve any moments that we may happen to possess! We gladly seize any opportunity to render Him, or those who are dear to Him, any little service, which, though in itself of small intrinsic worth, shows the sincerity of our thankfulness! The very mention of His name will cheer our hearts and lighten our faces. And if He is now no more, and has made it His dying request that, in a way that He has appointed, we should occasionally meet to remember Him and His service, how we should resent the idea of failing in the performance of such a sacred obligation!

These are the characteristics and expressions of true gratitude. And can we believe that where the manifestations are so different, the internal principle is still the same?

If the love of Christ is so languid in most nominal Christians, then their joy and trust in Him can hardly be expected to be very vigorous either. There is nothing distinctive or specific in their behaviour to indicate that they are sustained and animated by the hope of the Gospel.

The doctrine of the sanctifying work of the Holy Spirit appears to have fared still worse. Not merely are most Christians too little conscious of the inefficiency of their own unassisted endeavours to achieve heart and life holiness, but they fail to use daily the appointed means for the reception and cultivation of God's help. It is no exaggeration to state that for the most part their notions on this subject are so confused and faint that they can hardly be said to believe the doctrine at all.

It may be claimed that often the strongest pretence to religious belief has little or no basis in reality. Even excluding instances of blatant hypocrisy, claims of religious affection have been merely the product of a lively imagination, or the working of a fevered brain so that, in particular, this love of the Saviour dwells only in the disordered mind of the enthusiast. Furthermore, that religion's nature is more steady and rejects with scorn the support of mere indeterminate, trivial and useless feelings, such feelings vary in different men, and even in the same man at different times, according to the whim of their emotional state.

As for the operations of the Holy Spirit, it may probably be further urged that it is scarcely worthwhile spending much time in enquiring into the theory, when in practice, clearly there is no sure criterion whereby one can ascertain their reality, even in one's own life, much less in that of another. There has never been any shortage of those who lay claim to exceptional interventions in their lives, stretching the credulity of the ignorant and trying the patience of the wise. The doctrine, to say the best of it, can only serve to favour man's indolence. It is therefore wiser to give ourselves to that which is more solid and practical, such as setting right disordered passions and implanting and cultivating moral virtues. You are contending for what is not only altogether unworthy of our Master, but has made considerate men treat His religion with suspicion and disrepute. Under a show of honouring Him it in fact injures and discredits His cause. Warming as he proceeds, our objector will perhaps assume a more impatient tone. 'Have not these doctrines,' he exclaims 'been used as the basis for some of the most disgraceful actions in the name of Jesus?' If you want an example look at the Inquisition, in particular the Dominicans torturing their miserable victims for the love of Christ.

Objections discussed

Sadly, it has to be admitted that also the sacred name of religion has been prostituted for the most detestable ends by furious bigots, bloody persecutors and self-interested hypocrites of all types falsely calling themselves Christians. We readily admit that the teaching about spiritual and supernatural interventions has almost always been disgraced by the pretences and extravagant behaviour of fanatics and enthusiasts. All this, however, is simply another instance of man's depravity perverting God's bounty. Why is it here only that there is danger of abuse? There are many other examples both in the natural and moral world. Take for an instance the powers and properties of matter. Designed by Providence for our comfort and well-being, they are often misapplied to trifling ends and still more frequently turned into agents of misery and death. If religion were discarded, liberty would remain to plague the world. A power which, when well employed is the dispenser of light and happiness, has often, when abused, become infinitely mischievous. So if you extinguish liberty you blot out courage, and proceed to extinguish, one by one, reason, speech, memory and all man's discriminating prerogatives. Enough has been said in reply to an objection as indefensible as that which would equally warrant our condemning any physical or moral faculty altogether, because of its occasional abuse.

It must be admitted partly that there is no way whereby

the genuineness of religious emotions may be tested. We are not able always to read men's hearts and discover their real characters. Hence we do in some measure lie open to false and hypocritical claims which are made so triumphantly. But these claims do not prove that all similar ones are false and hypocritical any more than false claims to wisdom and honesty prove that there can be no such thing as a wise or honest man. We only argue in this way when our reason is corruptly biased. It is just as Jesus Himself taught us to expect. When the old problem is stated, 'Sir, didn't you sow good seed in your field? Where then did the weeds come from?' His own answer furnishes the best solution, 'An enemy did this' (Matt. 13:27–8). Hypocrisy is indeed detestable, and enthusiasm sufficiently mischievous to justify our being guarded about it. Yet we are apt to lay too much emphasis on appearances when we make our judgments. The manner and speech in which an uneducated man will express himself on the subject of religion will probably be uneducated. And better educated people may find it difficult not to be shocked. But we should endeavour not to make superficial judgments and should learn to recognise the genuineness of the individual, even though disguised by an uncultured manner.

Section II
On the admission of the passions into religion

The objection that by insisting on our obligation to make our Saviour the object of our religious feelings we are degrading the worship of the mind and understanding, and are substituting instead a set of mere feelings needs to be considered seriously. If it is right then it is decisive; for ours must unquestionably be a 'spiritual act of worship' (Rom. 12:1).

This idea of our feelings being out of place in religion is an opinion which is very prevalent. There is partly a language problem here which has aggravated the situation. The result is that the form of religion which is opposite to

41

the warm and affectionate kind has become known as 'rational'. But this claim should not be too hastily admitted. Thorough and impartial discussion will, I believe, show it to be a gross and pernicious error.

An important defect in this teaching is that it proposes to exclude at once from the service of religion a most important part of man's make-up. It condemns as worse than useless all the most active and constructive principles of our nature. Surely, like the body's organs, so the elementary qualities and original passions of the mind were all given to us for good reason by an all-wise Creator. One of the sad evidences of our fallen nature is that these emotions are now perpetually rebelling against the powers of reason and conscience, to which they should be subject. But even if revelation had been silent on the matter, natural reason might have presumed, to some degree, that a religion come from God would completely repair the consequences of our depravity. Mere human wisdom had, indeed, tacitly confessed that this was a task beyond it. Of the two most celebrated systems of philosophy, the one expressly confirmed the usurpation of the passions, while the other, despairing of ever being able to regulate them, saw nothing left but to extinguish them. Not so Christianity, whose peculiar glory and main office is to bring all the faculties of our nature into their just subordination and dependence so that the whole man, functionally complete, may be restored to the true purpose of his existence and be devoted to God's service and glory. 'Love the Lord your God with all your heart' (Luke 10:27) – such is the direct and comprehensive claim made on us in Scripture.

We can hardly look anywhere in the Bible without finding evidence that it is a religion involving the feelings that God particularly requires. Love, zeal, gratitude, joy, hope, trust, are each specified not as weaknesses, but urged upon us as our bounden duty, and commended as our acceptable worship. Passages are too numerous to quote. Let it suffice to refer the reader to the word of God. He will observe there that as the use of the emotions towards their legitimate object is always praised, so a cold, hard, unfeeling heart is condemned. Lukewarmness is seen as the object of God's disgust and aversion while zeal and love those of His favour and delight. The taking away of a stony heart and its replacement by a warmer and more tender nature is the promised result of His returning favour and renewing grace.

Paul's prayer on behalf of the Philippian Christians was 'that your love may abound more and more' (Phil. 1:9). When engaged in their favourite work of celebrating the goodness of their Saviour, their souls appear to burn within them, while their hearts are kindled to rapture. Language is inadequate as they call the whole of nature to unite in hallelujahs of gratitude, joy and praise. When it pleased God to check the future Apostle of the Gentiles in his wild career, and to make him an outstanding example of transforming grace, was the strength of his feelings diminished? It was not simply that the direction of them was changed. He brought his entire and unabated affections into the service of his Master. His zeal now burned with an increased brightness whose ardour no intenseness or prolongation of suffering could allay. Finally the worship and service of the departed spirits in heaven's glory is not represented as a cold intellectual exercise, but as the worship and service of gratitude and love.

It is prudent here to guard against the mistaken idea that the strength of religious feelings is to be estimated mainly by the degree of purely animal fervour, excitement, etc., which depends much upon an individual's temperament. It is often apparent that people with certain dispositions may work themselves up into a state of passion without much difficulty, while their heart is by no means truly or deeply interested. High degrees of passion may be felt by bad men, while good men entirely lack them. They may be put on, they may be genuine, but whether genuine or put on they do not form the true standard by which the real nature or strength of religious feeling is to be determined.

To verify these points, we must try to find out whether they appear to be grounded in true knowledge, with their root in strong and just concepts, or whether they are based on ignorance. Are they natural and easy, or constrained and forced? Are they awake with their thoughts fixed on important issues, taking pleasure in their nourishment by prayer, praise and religious contemplation, or do they avoid such occasions when they are offered? We must note whether these religious feelings are only an occasional experience or a continuous one for the soul. Have they mastery over vicious passions and weaknesses? We must also note whether they moderate and control those appetites and desires which are only blameworthy in excess. Above all, we must examine how these characteristics show themselves in the discharge of the ordinary duties of life, viz. in personal, domestic, relative, professional, social and civil duties. Their wide range and universal influence will usually distinguish them from those partial efforts of hard work and self-denial, to which man is prompted by subordinate motives. Proofs not deduced from conduct are in some degree ambiguous. This, however, whether we argue from reason or from Scripture, is a certain criterion. From daily incidents of married and domestic life, we learn that warm affection, occasionally vehement, but superficial and transitory can be consistent with conduct which shows incontestable evidence of neglect and unkindness.

But the emotion which alone is dignified by Scripture with the name of love, is a deep, not a superficial feeling. It is fixed and permanent, not an occasional emotion. It proves the genuineness of its name by actions which correspond with its nature, by efforts to gratify the wishes and to promote the interests of the object of its affection. 'If anyone loves me, he will obey my teachings' (John 14:23). 'This is love for God: to obey his commands' (1 John 5:3). This then is the best standard by which to test the quality, or estimate the strength, of religious feelings. Without allowing ourselves to become too complacent as a result of temporary fervours, we should carefully and frequently test ourselves by impartially examining our daily conduct and regularly comparing our actual achievements with our possible ones.

We readily concede to the objector, whose arguments we

are considering, that religious feelings must be expected to vary between people and in the same individual at different times, according to natural temper, age, situation and conditions. But to found an objection on this ground would be as unreasonable as it would be to deny our obligation to obey the teaching to relieve the needy on the grounds that people's infinitely varying circumstances must render it impossible to specify beforehand the sum which each individual ought on the whole to allot to this purpose. To both cases we may apply the maxim of an eminent writer: 'An honest heart is the best casuist.' He who in everything except religion is warm and animated, can hardly expect that his plea on the ground of natural temper should be accepted, any more than that of a person who should use his own poverty as a justification for not relieving the wants of the needy at the very time when he is embarking on unbridled expenditure on his own account. In both cases it is the willing mind that is required. Where that is found 'the gift is acceptable according to what one has, not according to what he does not have' (2 Cor. 8:12).

These decisive proofs taken from God's word, which show the unreasonableness of the objections to showing any emotion in religion, would make further arguments appear superfluous to anyone who accepts the authority of Scripture. Yet the point is so important and so little regarded that it may not be amiss to continue the discussion. The best results of our understanding will be found to fall in with what is the authoritative language of revelation and to call in the assistance of the feelings in religion's service will prove to be not only what common sense permits, but also to be that which our natural condition indispensably requires. We all have a work to complete which involves our eternal interests and it is a work to which we are not naturally disposed. We live in a world full of objects which distract our attention and divert our endeavours, and a deadly enemy is always on hand to seduce and beguile us. If we persevere, then success is around, but our efforts must be unremitting. There is a call on us for vigorous and continual resolution, self-denial and activity. Now man is not a being of mere intellect. The slightest arousal of an appetite is often enough to divert us to behave in a manner contrary to our clearest judgment, our highest interest and most resolute determinations. Sickness, poverty, disgrace and even eternal misery itself are all excluded from view, pushed beyond the field of vision by some poor, insubstantial, transient object, so minute and contemptible as almost to escape the notice of the eye of reason.

This applies more to our religious concerns than to any other, because here the interests at stake are of transcendent importance. But they hold equally in every circumstance where there is a call for laborious, painful and continued effort from which one is likely to be deterred by obstacles, or seduced by pleasing attractions. What then should be done when involved in any such arduous and necessary undertaking? The answer is obvious – endeavour, not only to convince the mind, but also to involve the heart. To procure, you will need the help of the emotions. This course would be followed naturally by anyone knowing that someone in whom he had a deep interest (a child for instance, or a brother) were about to enter on a long, difficult, perilous and critical adventure, in which success would mean honour and affluence, while defeat contempt and ruin. And still more, if the parent were convinced that his child possessed the faculties which rightly applied would prove equal to all the exigences of the enterprise, but knew him also to be volatile and wavering and so had reason to doubt his resolution and his vigilance; how that parent would endeavour so to grip his child's mind with the worth and dignity of the undertaking, that there would be no room for lesser considerations!

It was an unerring observer who remarked, 'For the people of this world are more shrewd in dealing with their own kind than are the people of the light' (Luke 16:8). In religion it is a fact that we have to argue and plead with men for principles of action, whose wisdom and expediency are universally acknowledged in worldly matters. The case which has been just described, is a true but faint representation of our condition in this life. Frail and infirm of purpose, we have a business to carry out which is supremely important. Temptations to neglect it abound, difficulties and dangers are numerous and urgent and the night that death brings comes at any time 'when no-one can work' (John 9:4). It seems to be a situation where one needs a powerful stimulant. Mere knowledge on its own is not enough. The feelings remain to supply the deficiency. They meet the occasion precisely and suit the purposes intended. Yet, when we propose to fit ourselves for our great undertaking by calling them to our aid, we are told that we are acting contrary to reason. Is this reasonable, first to remove our armour and then to send us to the sharpest of encounters? To summon us to the severest labours, but first to rob us of the nourishment which should brace our sinews and summon up strength?

And now, if the place of feelings in religion has been shown to be reasonable it will not require many words to demonstrate that it is our Saviour who is the proper object of them. We know that love, gratitude, joy, hope, trust (the feelings in question) all have their appropriate objects. It must be conceded, of course, that if these appropriate objects are not to be seen then it is perfectly unreasonable to expect that the corresponding emotion would be aroused. If we ask for love, for an object which is not excellent or desirable, for gratitude, where there is no obligation, for joy without justification of it, for hope where nothing is expected or for trust where there are no grounds for it, then, indeed, we are in grave error. It would be Egyptian slavery, indeed, to demand the product without first providing the wherewithal to make it. Is it a fact then that we are ready to adopt the language of our Saviour's avowed enemies and say to Him in whom 'all the fulness of the Deity lives in bodily form' (Col. 2:9) that 'He had no beauty or majesty to attract us to him. Nothing in his appearance that we should desire him' (Isa. 53:2)? Are we under no obligation to the one who 'being in very nature God, did not consider equality with God something to be grasped, but made himself nothing, taking the very nature of a servant, being made in human likeness. And being found in appearance as a man, he humbled himself and became obedient to death – even death on a cross!' (Phil. 2:6–8). Are we not joyful that 'a Saviour has been born' (Luke 2:11) through whom we may 'share in the inheritance of the saints in the kingdom of light. For he has rescued us from the dominion of darkness and brought us into the kingdom of the Son he loves' (Col. 1:12–13). Can there be a hope comparable to the one 'to which he has called you' (Eph. 1:18), 'which is Christ in you, the hope of glory' (Col. 1:27)? Can our confidence be placed other than on 'Jesus Christ [who] is the same yesterday and today and for ever' (Heb. 13:8)? Surely, if our opponent is not void of emotion, he will blush with shame and indignation when he examines his objections honestly.

Section III
Consideration of the reasonableness of affections towards an invisible being

While compelled to acknowledge that religious feelings can be felt for our Saviour, our disputant maintains that by our very constitution we cannot experience such feelings for one who is invisible, and this because we are shut off from all the usual means of communication and intercourse, which forge links between individuals.

There is certainly something in this argument. It might even seem that the authority of Scripture was in its favour – 'For anyone who does not love his brother, whom he has seen, cannot love God, whom he has not seen' (1 John 4:20). Visible objects certainly leave stronger and more lasting impressions on us than do invisible ones. While accepting that the conditions make it more difficult to preserve the feelings that we are discussing in a strong and vigorous state, is it impossible? Such a conclusion would be most precipitate and anyone disposed to accept it would be well advised to remember that the argument applies equally against the possibility of our loving God, which is a duty laid upon every believer. But we need only look back at the Scriptures already quoted to be convinced that religious feelings are taught and urged upon us as a serious duty for all believers. Assuming that we are not devoid of the principles of love, gratitude, joy, hope and trust then they must be aroused in us as we contemplate the various aspects of our Saviour. Peter could say in truth to Christians, 'Though you have not seen him, you love him; and even though you do not see him now, you believe in him and are filled with an inexpressible and glorious joy' (1 Pet. 1:8).

Our Saviour is not far from us; our relationship with Him is such that we can be in continuous contact and communication. We must not think of Him as being incapable of entering into our little concerns, and sympathising with them; for we are assured that He is not one 'who is unable to sympathise with our weaknesses, but we have one who has been tempted in every way, just as we are' (Heb. 4:15). The pictures used to describe Him are such as to convey the idea of extreme tenderness. 'He tends his flock like a shepherd: He gathers the lambs in his arms and carries them close to his heart; he gently leads those that have young' (Isa. 40:11). 'They will neither hunger nor thirst, nor will the desert heat or the sun beat upon them. He who has compassion on them will guide them and lead them beside springs of water' (Isa. 49:10). 'I will not leave you as orphans' was one of His last words of comfort (John 14:18). The children of Christ are denied a personal view of Him, but are not separated from His fatherly love and care. So let them be kept alert and vigilant by the exciting prospect of that blessed day when He has promised, 'I will come back and take you to be with me' (John 14:3). Then they will be admitted into His nearer presence: 'Now we see but a poor reflection . . . then we shall see face to face. Now I know in part; then I shall know fully even as I am fully known' (1 Cor. 13:12).

But more than enough has been said to prove that this particular case, from its very nature, provided ample reasons and means for rousing the emotions and it might be argued that by diligent and habitual application we might

49

seek to increase our feelings towards our Saviour. But, the most important point has been left to the last, which is the fact that the Christian's hope is founded not on the speculations or the strength of man, but on the declaration of Him who cannot lie, and who is Almighty.

Scripture tells us that part of the operations of the Holy Spirit is to implant these heavenly principles in the human mind and to cherish their growth. We are encouraged to believe that, in answer to our prayers, this assistance from above will make our endeavours fruitful if made in humble dependence on God's grace. We may therefore with confidence take the means which have been suggested.

Let us now consider real Christians, those who have actually proved the truth of our arguments. They have not simply assumed the title, but have made a commitment and experienced the power of Christ in their lives. Love flows in their hearts towards their Redeemer. It is a love which is not superficial and lacking in meaning, but constant and rational, resulting from a strong sense of the worth of its object, and increased by an abiding sense of unworthiness. It shows itself in acts of careful obedience or patient suffering. Such was the religion of the holy martyrs in the sixteenth century. They realised the theory which we have briefly traced. Look at their writings and you will find that their thoughts and feelings had been much strengthened by regular contemplation of Jesus. They used the required means. What was the result? Persecution and distress, degradation and contempt assailed them, but in vain, for these evils served but to bring their feelings closer to the one they worshipped. And their love, far from diminishing or being extinguished, rose to all the exigences of the occasion, and burned with increased ardour. When at last brought forth to a cruel and ignominious death, they did not complain at their fate, but rather rejoiced that they were counted worthy to suffer for Christ's name. The writer might refer to more recent times, but let us rather look at the apostles. A cursory perusal of their writings shows that they commend and even prescribe to us the love of Christ as one of the chief Christian graces. A closer inspection of those writings reveals abundant proofs that they were themselves shining examples of their teaching. Our Saviour was truly the object of their warmest feelings, and what He had done and suffered on their behalf, a matter for continual and grateful remembrance.

The bulk of nominal Christians are disposed to form a religious system for themselves, instead of taking it from the word of God, and it is notable that they scarcely admit, except in the most vague and general terms, the doctrine covering the effects of the Holy Spirit. When we look at Scripture for information on this point we find a very different story. We are taught that of ourselves we can do nothing, that we are by nature children of wrath and under the power of the evil spirit, our understandings being naturally dark and our hearts averse from spiritual things. We are directed to pray for the influence of the Holy Spirit to enlighten our understanding, to dissipate our prejudices, to purify our corrupt minds, and to renew us after the image of our heavenly Father. It is this influence which is represented as wakening us from sleep, enlightening our spiritual darkness, as quickening us when dead (Eph. 2:1, 5), as rescuing us from the dominion of darkness, as drawing us to God, as bringing 'us into the kingdom of the Son he loves' (Col. 1:13), as 'created in Christ Jesus' (Eph. 2:10), as dwelling in us and walking in us (2 Cor. 6:16), so that taking off our old self with its practices, we are to consider ourselves as having 'put on the new self, which is being renewed in knowledge in the image of its Creator' (Col. 3:10), and as those who are to be 'a dwelling in which God lives by his Spirit' (Eph. 2:22). It is only by God's help that we can grow in grace and holiness. The word of God teaches these particular lessons so repeatedly that there can hardly be room for a difference of opinion among those who accept its authority.

Section IV
Inadequate conceptions entertained by nominal Christians of the terms of acceptance with God

It seems then that contrary to Scripture's plainest dictates, the Church's ritual, the Holy Spirit's sanctifying work, the first fruits of our reconciliation to God, our purchase by our Saviour's death, and His best gift to His future disciples – it seems that these marvellous things are undervalued and slighted. As was shown earlier, our thoughts of our Saviour are confused and faint, our feelings towards Him are languid and lukewarm, and quite inappropriate for those who have been rescued from ruin at such a price and endowed with a sight of eternal glory. Our feelings do not compare with those felt by others, ransomed from the same ruin and partakers of the same inheritance. If this is true let us not close our eyes to our real state, but rather endeavour to trace the evil to its source. We should examine carefully the foundations of our faith. If these are unsound and hollow, then the building cannot be safe, whatever its external appearance.

The question has to be asked on the subject of the means of a sinner's acceptance by God, whether there is not reason to suspect that nominal Christians to whom we have been referring entertain very superficial, confused and, indeed, highly dangerous ideas. With little more than a faint and nominal reference to the one who 'bore our sins in his own body on the tree' (1 Pet. 2:24), they rest their eternal hopes on a vague, general assumption of God's unqualified mercy. Still more erroneously, they may rely largely on their own negative or positive merits in such terms. 'They can look upon their lives with an impartial eye, and congratulate themselves on their inoffensiveness in society; on their having been exempt, at least, from any gross vice, or if sometimes accidentally betrayed into it, on its never having been a habit; yet the balance is in their favour, or, not much against them, when their good and bad actions are weighed fairly, and due allowance is made for human frailty.' These considerations largely suffice to calm their apprehensions in moments of serious thought, or occasional dejection, and sometimes perhaps when they are less complacent, they also call to their aid the memory of God's unbounded mercy and pity. These people, however, would not disclaim the Saviour, or relinquish their title to a share in the benefits of His death. They end their prayers with the name of Christ. But if this is not from habit, or from conformity to the established faith, perhaps it has something of the ambiguity which influenced the dying philosopher when he ordered the customary mark of homage to be paid to the god of medicine.

There are many shades of difference between those who flatly renounce and those who cordially embrace the doctrine of Christ's redemption. There are those who have a sort of general, indeterminate and ill-understood dependence on our Saviour. But their hopes, so far as they can be discerned, appear to be founded ultimately on the persuasion that they have, through Christ, become members of a new dispensation, wherein they will be tried more leniently. God will not be too severe in marking wrongdoing, but He will dispense with the stricter demands of His law, which are too strict for us frail creatures to hope to fulfil. Christianity has moderated the demands of divine justice and all that is now required of us, is that thankfully we trust in the merits of Christ for the pardon of our sins, and the acceptance of our sincere though imperfect obedience. The frailties and infirmities to which our nature is liable, or to which life exposes us, will be judged severely and since practice really determines character, we may rest assured that if on the whole our lives are tolerably good, we shall escape with little or no punishment, and through Jesus Christ our Lord, shall partake finally of heavenly felicity.

It is not feasible to fathom the human heart, and therefore we should always speak with caution and diffidence when affirming the existence of any internal principles and feelings from external appearances or declarations. But it is sometimes not difficult to one familiar with the make-up of the human mind to discern that, in general, people who use this language rely not so much on the merits of Christ and the assistance of His grace as on their own ability to fulfil the moderated requirement of justice. Hence He will find them disposed rather to extenuate the severity of their disease than to magnify the excellence of the proffered remedy. He will find them apt to gloss over those things in themselves which they cannot fully justify, and highlight what they believe to be their good qualities and commendable actions in order to balance the good against the bad. If the result is not very unfavourable, then they consider that they will be entitled to claim the benefits of our Saviour's sufferings as a matter of course. They have no conception of the importance or difficulty of the duty to which Scripture refers, to 'submit to God's righteousness' (Rom. 10:3), or of our tendency to seek to justify ourselves in His sight, rather than to acknowledge ourselves to be guilty and helpless sinners. All these errors result naturally from the mistaken conception held regarding the fundamental principles of Christianity. They do not consider Christianity to be a means for justifying 'the wicked' (Rom. 4:5), by Christ's dying for them while still His enemies (Rom. 5:6, 8), a means for reconciling us to God and making the fruits of holiness the result and not the cause of our justification and reconciliation.

In short, it freely opens the door of God's mercy to all penitent sinners, so that obeying the impulse of which God's grace awakened them from the sleep of death and moved them to seek forgiveness, they enter and through the regenerating influence of the Holy Spirit are enabled to bring forth the fruits of righteousness. Rather they conceive of Christianity as being the opening of the door of mercy for those who on the grounds of their own merits could not have hoped to justify themselves before God. However this may yet be admitted for Christ's sake, because they have previously satisfied the modified requirements of divine justice. In speaking to others about the Gospel they are apt to dwell too much on the part that we play and which entitles us to a part in the benefit of Christ's sufferings instead of stating clearly that the benefits of

Christ's death are extended to us freely 'without money and without cost' (Isa. 55:1).

The practical consequences of these errors are as might be expected. That feeling which we should experience of our natural misery and helplessness tends to be lacking as does that deep sense of gratitude for the sufferings, merits and intercession of Christ, on which our reconciliation to God depends. They regard it more as a contract between two parties, in which each independently has his own distinct condition to carry out. Man must do his duty while God, for His part, will justify and accept man for Christ's sake. If man does not fail in the discharge of his condition, then he can be sure that God, for His part, will be faithful in His. What we find is that those who represent the Gospel scheme in this way reveal the subject which most fills their hearts by their proneness to give purely moral discourses which either fail to mention or at most give only a passing reference to their Redeemer's sufferings and love. Their Saviour's name does not set them on fire and unlike the apostles they are in no danger of being betrayed by their fervour into an untimely discourse on the riches of His unutterable mercy. When addressing those whom they consider to have sinful habits and under God's wrath, they advise them to mend their ways in preparation for coming to Christ, instead of exhorting them to throw themselves in penitence at the foot of the cross, where they can obtain pardon and find grace to help in time of need.

The importance of the subject that we have discussed cannot be overstated and no one should mistake our meaning. The important question is, where do we place our dependence for pardon and for holiness? Surely the holding of this prevailing error concerning the nature of the Gospel explains the widespread tepid feelings expressed towards our Saviour which we have already referred to, also the inadequate awareness of the necessity and value of the Holy Spirit's help. Even if these people of whom we have been thinking do basically rely on the atonement of Christ, yet in their scheme of things the object at which they are most accustomed to look, from which they gain most satisfaction is not the sufferings and atoning death of a crucified Saviour, but their own merits and service. The feelings towards our Lord cannot be expected to flourish because they do not receive what they require to nourish them and encourage their growth. If we should love Him as warmly and rejoice in Him as triumphantly as the first Christians then we must, like them, learn to place our full trust in Him, and say with the apostle, 'May I never boast except in the cross of our Lord Jesus Christ' (Gal. 6:14) – 'who has become for us wisdom from God – that is, our righteousness, holiness and redemption' (1 Cor. 1:30).

Doubtless many, to their eternal ruin, have abused the doctrine of salvation by grace, vainly trusting in Christ for pardon and acceptance, while their lives of vice have plainly proved their pretensions to be groundless. The tree is to be known by its fruits and there are good grounds to doubt the presence of true faith when the fruits of holiness are not in evidence. How dreadful at the last day to have to hear our Saviour say, 'I never knew you. Away from me, you evildoers!' (Matt. 7:23). But the danger of error on this side ought not to blind us to the opposite one. The writer of this work would contend that those who in the main accept the doctrines of the Church of England, must agree that our dependence on our Saviour, as the only grounds for our acceptance with God, and the means of all its fruits and glorious consequences, must not be a mere formality, but real and genuine. '. . . turn to God in repentance and have faith in our Lord Jesus' (Acts 20:21) was the sum of the apostle's instructions. It is not an occasional invocation or a transient recognition of the name and authority of Christ, that goes to make up what we understand as believing in Jesus. This is no easy task and if we trust that we do believe, then we do well to cry out with the imploring suppliant 'help me overcome my unbelief' (Mark 9:24). Deeply conscious of our guilt and misery, heartily repenting of our sins and firmly resolving to forsake them, we must rest entirely on the merit of the crucified Redeemer for our hopes of escape from the punishment which we deserve and for our deliverance from their enslaving power. This must be our first, our last, our only plea. We are to surrender ourselves up to Him who 'has freed us from our sins by his blood' (Rev. 1:5) to be sanctified by His Spirit, resolving to receive Him as our Lord and Master, and learn in His school to obey all His commandments.

We should like to focus our attention on those who believe vaguely in the death of Christ, as the satisfaction for our sins and for the purchase of our future happiness, and in the sanctifying influence of the Holy Spirit. These they accept as fundamental articles of faith, yet see these doctrines as being so much above us as to be beyond our comprehension. We should look more at the Gospel's practical and moral precepts they say. 'Our nature is frail and our temptations strong and numerous, so that by reducing Gospel morality to its practice we shall find plenty to occupy us. Attention to moral precepts, rather than to the mysterious doctrines which you are urging upon us, will ensure that we are prepared to appear before God the judge when the time comes.' This argument is dismantled with ease by reference to Christ's words and those of His beloved disciple. 'The work of God is this: to believe in the one he has sent' (John 6:29). 'And this is his command: to believe in the name of his Son, Jesus Christ' (1 John 3:23). But a moment's consideration shows how absurd this argument is. It is in fact the language of Unitarians who might argue this: 'Why all this expensive and complicated machinery? It is so unlike the simplicity of nature, and unworthy of God's hand. It even offends against the rules of propriety which are required to be observed in the imperfect compositions of the human intellect.'

Well may the Socinian assume this lofty tone with those whom we are now addressing. If we are discussing revealed truths then common sense suggests that from their nature and size they deserve our most serious consideration. It is the teaching of Epicurus to admit the existence of these 'heavenly things', but to deny that there is any connection with human concerns, or influence on human actions. Such a viewpoint is not only unreasonable, but also profane in treating as matters of lesser importance those parts of

Christian belief which make such a strong call on our reverence by the dignity of the one of whom they relate.

The irreverence of this view is nowhere more striking than in its ingratitude. Scripture affirms that our Saviour is 'the radiance of God's glory and the exact representation of his being, sustaining all things by his powerful word' (Heb. 1:3). We go on from this to consider the purpose of His coming to earth and all that He did and suffered for us. Surely we are guilty of gross ingratitude in our repeated failure for whatever reason to contemplate these miracles of mercy. For those whose minds will only respond to fear that motive is also added in that we are plainly warned, both directly and indirectly, by the Jewish nation's example, that God will not exonerate those who disregard His signal acts of condescension and kindness. But since this is a question of pure revelation, arguments from probability may not be considered decisive. We must appeal to revelation. In the interests of time and space we refer the reader to the sacred writings themselves for complete satisfaction. We strongly recommend him to weigh with the utmost seriousness those passages of Scripture which set out Christian doctrine. Those who hold the view which we are combating will by this means be convinced that their religion is un-Scriptural. They will learn, instead of turning their eyes away from the majestic features of Christianity, always to keep these in view, as the first principles from which all the rest derive their origin and receive their best support.

Let each of us solemnly ask ourselves whether we have fled for refuge to the appointed hope. And whether we are regularly looking to it as the only source of consolation. We read, 'For no-one can lay any foundation other than the one already laid' (1 Cor. 3:11). There is no other ground to depend upon; no other plea for pardon. But here there is hope which is complete. Let us so strive that our hearts may experience a deep conviction of our need of a Redeemer, and of the value of the mediation He offers. Let us humbly fall down before God's throne imploring His pity and pardon in the name of His beloved Son. Let us beg for a true spirit of repentance and an undivided faith in the Lord Jesus. Let us not be satisfied till the sincerity of our belief is confirmed to us in the way characterised by the apostle that 'to you who believe, this stone is precious' (1 Pet. 2:7). Let us also strive daily to increase in love towards our Saviour and pray earnestly that we may be filled 'with all joy and peace as you trust in him, so that you may overflow with hope by the power of the Holy Spirit' (Rom. 15:13). Let us be diligent in following the instructions already given for cherishing and cultivating Christ's love. To this end let us work assiduously to increase our knowledge, so that our love may be deeply rooted and rational. By meditating frequently on the incidents in our Saviour's life, and still more on the astonishing circumstances of His death; by often reminding ourselves of the state from which He proposes to rescue us, and the glories of His heavenly kingdom; by continuous contact with Him by prayer and praise, dependence and confidence in dangers, hope and joy in our brighter hours; in all these ways let us endeavour to keep Him constantly before our minds, and so render more distinct, lively and intelligent all our concepts of Him. The title of Christian is a reproach to us, if we are estranged from the one whose name we bear. The name of Jesus is not to be to us like that of Allah to a Muslim, a talisman or an amulet to be worn on the arm like a badge and symbol of our profession; something to preserve us from evil by some mysterious means. Rather it is to be engraved deeply on the heart by the finger of God in everlasting characters. It is our clear claim to present peace and future glory. The assurance which it brings of a bright inheritance will lighten the burdens and sorrows of life, and in happier moments, it will impart to us a taste of that fullness of joy which is at God's right hand so we shall be able to join on earth in the heavenly anthem 'Worthy is the Lamb, who was slain, to receive power and wealth and wisdom and strength and honour and glory and praise.' 'To him who sits on the throne and to the Lamb be praise and honour . . . for ever and ever!' (Rev. 5:13).

IV

ON THE PREVAILING INADEQUATE CONCEPTIONS CONCERNING THE NATURE AND THE STRICTNESS OF PRACTICAL CHRISTIANITY

Section I

It seems to be commonly accepted today that provided a man admits the truth of Christianity in general, even though he knows or considers little about its details, if he is not in the habit of committing any of the grosser vices against his fellow-creatures then there is no particular reason to be dissatisfied with him, or to question the genuineness of his claim of the name and privileges of a Christian. The title implies simply a formal assent to Christianity in general, a certain standard of moral behaviour, but little superior to what we expect from a good deist, Muslim, or Hindu.

Ask those who question whether this is a fair representation of the religion of the bulk of the Christian world what would happen if it were proved beyond dispute that Christianity is a mere forgery. Would this cause any great change in behaviour or thinking? Would any change come about as a result of this discovery, except in a few rash opinions, which are of little consequence, and in attendance of public worship, which it might still be thought better to do occasionally for example's sake? Their regard for their character, health, domestic and social comforts would still continue to restrain them from vicious excesses, and to prompt them to persist in the discharge of their various duties as at present. Would they in fact find themselves bereft of their repository of counsel and instruction, the rule of their conduct, their habitual source of peace, and hope, and consolation?

These questions are unnecessary for they are answered already by the lives of many unbelievers, between whom and these professed Christians, even familiar associates, men of discernment and observation, would discover little difference either in conduct or mental state. How little, then, does Christianity deserve the reputation of uniqueness and superiority with which it has been almost universally acclaimed! Not to mention its pre-eminence as a code of practice above all other systems of ethics! How unmerited are the praises which have been lavished upon it by its friends! Praises in which even its enemies, not in general disposed to make concessions in its favour, have acquiesced!

Was this why the Son of God condescended to become our teacher and example, so that we might tread in His steps? Was it for this that Christ's apostles submitted voluntarily to hunger, nakedness, pain, ignominy and death, having been forewarned to expect such treatment?

It may be objected that we are overlooking an observation which we ourselves have made, that Christianity has raised the general standard of morals, standards to which unbelievers now find it prudent to conform. While they avail themselves of the pure morality of Christianity, and try to take for themselves the credit for it, they at the same time stamp its authors as ignorant dupes or designing impostors!

But are Christianity's motives so unimportant for its practice that the one can be dispensed with while the other remains with undiminished force? Are its doctrines barren and inapplicable, or at least an unnecessary theory whose place would be well supplied by a more simple and less extravagant system? But is Christianity reduced to a mere creed? Is its practical influence limited by a few specious arguments? At root is it only a few speculative opinions and useless and unproductive dogmas? Is this the basis of that marvellous distinction which the evangelist made so unequivocally between those who accept and those who reject the Gospel: 'Whoever believes in the Son has eternal life, but whoever rejects the Son will not see life, for God's wrath remains on him' (John 3:36)?

The morality of the Gospel is not such a flimsy fabric. Christianity throughout shows proofs of its divine origin, and its practical teachings are as pure as its doctrines are sublime. Is it possible to find injunctions which are stricter in their limits yet more comprehensive in their scope than those with which the word of God abounds? 'And whatever you do, whether in word or deed, do it all in the name of the Lord Jesus' (Col. 3:17). 'Be holy, because I am holy' (1 Pet. 1:16). 'Be perfect, therefore, as your heavenly Father is perfect' (Matt. 5:48). We are instructed to be perfect in holiness and to go on to perfection.

These are the admonitions of Scripture and surely we cannot be satisfied with less. On the subject of the changes that occur when one becomes a real Christian, Scripture says, 'Everyone who has this hope in him purifies himself, just as he [God] is pure' (1 John 3:3).

True Christians are said to 'participate in the divine nature' (2 Pet. 1:4); to be created anew in the image of God; to be 'a temple of the Holy Spirit' (1 Cor. 6:19). The effects of which must appear 'in all goodness, righteousness and truth' (Eph. 5:9).

In spite of great progress made by Paul in all virtue, he still pressed on, 'Forgetting what is behind and straining towards what is ahead' (Phil. 3:13). For his disciples he prays that they may be 'filled to the measure of all the fulness of God' (Eph. 3:19), 'filled with the fruit of right- eousness' (Phil. 1:11), 'live a life worthy of the Lord and may please him in every way: bearing fruit in every good work' (Col. 1:10). Also from the wording of the Lord's Prayer we understand what our constant attitude should be, 'your will be done on earth as it is in heaven' (Matt. 6:10).

It is the characteristic feature of true Christians that, relying on Scripture's promises to repenting sinners of acceptance through the Redeemer, they have renounced all other masters, and unreservedly devoted themselves to God. Christians are the sworn enemies of sin, which they will allow in no form. The war against it is universal and irreconcilable.

Furthermore, they are now determined to yield themselves without reserve to the service of their rightful sovereign. They are not their own property for their bodily and mental faculties, natural and acquired endowments, substance, authority, time, influence, all these they consider as belonging to them, not for self-gratification, but as instruments to be consecrated to and employed in the service of God.

Thus it is Christianity's prerogative to 'take captive every thought to make it obedient to Christ' (2 Cor. 10:5). They who are aware of its power resolve in the words of Scripture to live no longer 'for themselves but for him who died for them' (2 Cor. 5:15); they know their own weaknesses, they know that the way they have before them is narrow and difficult, but they know too the encouraging assurance, that 'those who hope in the Lord will renew their strength' (Isa. 40:31), and relying on this inspiring declaration, they resolve that the maxim governing their future lives shall be to do 'all for the glory of God' (1 Cor. 10:31).

While Christ's servants remain in this life, however glorious the outcome of their work, they receive many humiliating reminders of their continuing imperfections. Daily they find reason to confess, that they cannot do the things that they would. Their determination, however, is unshaken, and it is the firm desire of their hearts to grow in all holiness. They are spurred on by the fear of failure. Where their all is at stake, they do not depend on feelings and impressions. Christ's example is their pattern and the word of God is their rule. There they read, that 'without holiness no-one will see the Lord' (Heb. 12:14). It is said of real Christians that they are 'being transformed into his likeness' (2 Cor. 3:18), and they dare not permit themselves to believe that their future is assured except so far as they can discern in themselves the growing evidence of this resemblance.

However it is not simply the fear of misery and the desire for happiness that prompts their endeavours to excel in holiness. They seek it for its own sake. Nor is it solely out of self-interest that they are influenced in their determination to obey God's will and cultivate His favour. This determination has its roots in a deep and humbling sense of His exalted majesty and infinite power, and of their own extreme inferiority and smallness combined with a conviction that it is their duty as His creatures, to submit in all things to the will of their Creator. But these impressions of awe are relieved and elevated by a feeling of admiration for the infinite perfections and friendliness of God's character. Animated by a confident though humble trust in His fatherly kindness and protection, and quickened by the thankful memories of immense and continually increasing burdens, this is a Christian's love for God! A love compounded of admiration, preference, hope, trust, joy and moderated by awful reverence, and alert with continuous thankfulness.

The principles which have been referred to above exist in varying degrees and proportions. Natural disposition, past circumstances and numberless other particulars, may give rise to a great difference in the mental disposition of different Christians. In one the love, in another fear of God may have the ascendancy, while it may be trust in one, and in another gratitude. Yet all share a common feeling for God's sovereignty, perfection, goodness and a humble hope in His favour. Common, too, is the desire for holiness, continual progress towards perfection, a humbling consciousness of their own unworthiness, and of their many remaining weaknesses which so often spoil the simplicity of their intentions, thwart the execution of their purer purposes and frustrate the resolutions made in their better moments.

But there may be some who while not opposing our conclusions may try to escape them. It may be found, that they are not of general application. However pure they may be in the case of some individuals they are not applicable to ordinary Christians. From these, surely, not so much will be expected. Here, perhaps, is a secret reference to that supposed mitigation of the requirements of divine law in the Christian dispensation, which was formerly noted. This is so important a point that it ought to be answered by the authority of Scripture.

In the first place, the precepts are expressed in the broadest and most general terms, and no persons are at liberty to consider themselves exempted from any obligation of them. In the next place, the precepts in question contain within themselves abundant proofs of their universal application, inasmuch as they are based upon circumstances and relations which are common to all Christians, and whose benefits not even our objectors, though they might evade the practical deductions from them, would be willing to relinquish their share of them. Christians are not their own property having been 'bought at a price' (1 Cor. 7:23). They should 'no longer live for themselves but for him who died for them' (2 Cor. 5:15). They are commanded to perform the most difficult duties. Scripture makes many references to the fact that Christians are God's children by adoption. In general they are known as the servants and the children of God, and are required to serve Him with the same obedient submission and willing, loving service associated with a loving family relationship.

Measure the impact of that well-known passage – 'Love the Lord your God with all your heart and with all your soul, and with all your strength, and with all your mind' (Luke 10:27). The injunction is emphasised in order to silence the sophist and to alert the most inconsiderate. The conclusion to which this passage forces us is confirmed strikingly by other Scriptures in which God's love is commended to the whole of a Christian church (1 Cor. 12:14); or alternatively the lack of it (1 John 3:17, Rom. 16:18, Phil. 3:19). In other Scriptures the fact that God's love is not the chief and ruling affection is used as evidence to disprove people's claim to be called Christians, or as being the same as denying it (2 Tim. 3:4). Do not be deceived by imagining that only complete renunciation of the wish to obtain God's favour is condemned here. God will not tolerate divided loyalty. A single heart and eye are expressly declared to be the indispensable requirement. Under the picture of amassing heavenly treasure we are ordered to make God's favour and service our chief pursuit. The reason being, 'For where your treasure is, there your heart will be also' (Matt. 6:21). It is on this principle that when speaking of particular sins, phrases used in Scripture suggest that their sinfulness lies in the fact that they deviate our hearts from the one who should be their central concern. Sins which we might think very different in their heinousness are classed together, because they all share this same characteristic.

Furthermore, this is applied not only to what we rightly regard as serious crimes but also to those actions which are not only lawful, but we are urged to perform. 'Anyone who loves his father or mother more than me,' says our Saviour, 'is not worthy of me; anyone who loves his son or daughter more than me is not worthy of me' (Matt. 10:37). The spirit of these injunctions harmonises with many places in Scripture where zeal for the honour of God is commended. It is also in tune with that strong expression of disgust and abhorrence with which the lukewarm are spoken of as being more loathsome and offensive than are open and avowed enemies.

Other examples illustrating this point are furnished by many passages of Scripture in which we are commanded to promote God's glory as our supreme and universal aim. Here the honour due to Him is declared to be that in which He will brook no competitor. To put the same things in a different way; all who have read the Scriptures must admit that idolatry is the wrong which rouses God's greatest resentment and receives His severest punishment. But do not let us be deceived. Idolatry does not consist in bowing the knee to idols so much as in the attitude of the mind which makes us feel towards them any of that love, reverence or gratitude which God rightly reserves for Himself. Whatever else deflects our heart from Him, holding our first interest and the chief place in our esteem and affections, that is no less an idol to us than an image of wood or stone. In Scripture, God's servant is commanded not to set up his idol in his heart and sensuality and covetousness are repeatedly termed idolatry. The same God who says, 'I will not give my glory to another, or my praise to idols' (Isa. 42:8) also says, 'Let not the wise man boast of his wisdom, or the strong man boast of his strength, or the rich man boast of his riches' (Jer. 9:23). '. . . no-one may boast before him' (1 Cor. 1:29). 'Let him who boasts boast in the Lord' (2 Cor. 10:17).

Let the great, the wise, the learned and the successful take these awe-inspiring declarations to heart. Such reflection will tend naturally to produce a disposition which honours God and assists man; a frame of mind composed of reverence, humility, gratitude and delighting to be engaged in the praises and service of the Lord.

It only remains to be remarked that here, as in the former instances, the characters of the righteous and of the wicked, as delineated in Scripture, exactly correspond with the representations which have been given of the Scripture injunctions.

The importance of this sincere unreserved devotion to God's glory and service to the character of the true Christian has been insisted on at considerable length, not only because of its extreme importance, but also because it seems to be a duty which is too generally overlooked.

Section II

Having attempted to establish its strictness, and to discover the essential character of true practical Christianity, let us investigate in more detail its practice among professed Christians.

Religion, as we have already agreed, may be compared with the planting of a vigorous and active principle in the heart, where its authority is accepted as supreme and from where it, by degrees, expels whatever is opposed to it, and so gradually brings all feelings and desires under its complete control.

But though the heart is its special abode, every attempt

and activity must admit to its presence. That which will not or cannot receive its sacred stamp is to be not only condemned, but also abstained from or abandoned. Like the principle of life, it communicates its influence to the smallest and remotest part of the body. But the notion about religion that many entertain seems to be altogether different. They certainly begin by accepting its clear prohibitions and by fencing off from the field of human action an area which, though its fruits are attractive to them, they have to admit that this is forbidden ground. Next, they assign to religion an area over which, according to their circumstances and views, it will have only limited jurisdiction, and, having done this, they consider that what remains is for them to do just as they please with. Religion can lay claim to only a specified proportion of their thoughts, time, fortune, influence, and value; the rest they think is now their own with which to do as they please. Having paid their tithes they consider that the demands of the Church are well satisfied, and surely they may be permitted to enjoy what she has left without molesting or interfering.

The greatest part of human actions is regarded as unimportant. If men are not guilty of gross sins, remember to discharge their religious duties and do not stray into the forbidden ground, then what more can be expected of them? Instead of keeping all sin at a distance, which is the only safe thing to do, they will tend not to care how near they approach what they consider to be the boundary line. If they have not actually passed it, then there is no harm done and no trespass. Thus, the free and active spirit of religion is checked, for she must keep to her prescribed limits, and every attempt to extend them will be resisted.

But this is not all. Since whatever can be gained from the religious field, or whatever can be annexed from the forbidden ground, will mean so much more land where men can wander, free from restriction or interference. As a result the space she occupies diminishes till it is scarcely discernible, while her spirit extinguished, her force destroyed, she becomes little more than the nominal possessor of the now much contracted area of influence.

This is an only too faithful picture of the general state of things. The promotion of God's glory and gaining His favour are no longer considered to be the objects of our greatest concern and effort, which furnishes us with a vigorous, regular and universal principle of action. Instead, we have become our own masters. The idea of an ongoing service is irksome and humiliating to us and we rejoice that we are emancipated from it. Our attitude to life and all its possessions undergoes a total change. Whatever we have, we regard as our property rather than held on trust. If there does still exist a memory of a superior claim, then we are satisfied to make an occasional nominal acknowledgment of that fact.

This is why those who possess high rank, or great abilities, or wealth, or other means or instruments of usefulness, seem to have so little sense of responsibility. The instructive admonitions, 'Give an account of your management' (Luke 16:2), 'Put this money to work . . . until I come back' (Luke 19:13) are forgotten. If it is acknowledged that reference is to be made to a higher principle than that of our own pleasure then at best it will be the good of society or the welfare of our families. Even then the obligations which result from these relations are enforced on us by no higher sanction than that of family comfort and worldly interest. Besides all this there are many people without families or of private means, or living in retirement, to whom they can scarcely be held to apply! Accordingly, we find that most people in the upper strata of society in planning their studies, in the choice of residence, in how they spend their time, in their thoughts, conversation, and amusements, consider themselves at liberty, if no sin is involved, to consider their own pleasure.

The generous and alert spirit of Christian benevolence, looking everywhere for opportunities to serve, is thus exploded, and a system of decent selfishness is set up in its place. A system to be shunned for its impiety and abhorred because of lack of awareness to opportunities of spreading happiness.

But no man has a right to be idle. Not to mention the great work that we all must accomplish (and surely in the light of eternity the whole attention of a short and precarious life should be given), there are many things that those with health, leisure and wealth may find to do. Will ambition and greed never rest? Will there always be objects on which to fasten? Will the benevolence of Christians want for something to do?

Yet life rolls by, for too many of us, a course of 'shapeless idleness'. Recreations of one sort or another are its main interest. Even old age often finds us going the same round of amusements on which we embarked in our early youth. Meanwhile, since we are not giving in to any flagrant vice, and maybe neither are we neglecting religious observances, we persuade ourselves that we have no need to feel uneasy. On the whole, we do not fall below the general moral standard and we can therefore allow ourselves to glide downstream without fear of the consequences.

Some seem to take up sensual pleasures. Their chief happiness consists in one form or other of animal pleasure. We are thinking not of those who renounce all pretence to the name of Christians, but of those who maintain a certain decency of character and perhaps are moderately observant of the forms of religion. Such should be termed sober sensualists. 'Put to death, therefore, whatever belongs to your earthly nature' (Col. 3:5) is the Christian precept; but a soft luxurious path of regular self-indulgence is the practice of most modern Christians. The constant control and discipline brought by restraint and self-denial, and which are necessary in order to prevent the unnoticed invasion by unworthy desires, seem to be no longer used.

Those who profess to be Christians are called to diligent watchfulness and active service. But those people to whom we have been referring forget the duties that they owe to themselves and also to their fellow-creatures and act as though their lives consisted of a state of uniform indulgence, and vacant, unprofitable sloth. To increase the comforts of wealth, to provide for the gratification of appetite, to enjoy luxuries without disease, and indolence without lassitude, seems the chief study of their lives. There are also those in this class, who, by substituting the means for the end, make the preservation of health and spirits not a means to usefulness, but as a source of pleasure in itself.

Just as there is sober sensuality, so there is also sober greed and sober ambition. The chief sphere of their influence is the commercial and professional world. They are often recognised and openly affirmed as master principles of action. But where this is not the case then they assume such plausible forms, are called by such specious names and produce such powerful arguments that they are cordially received and permitted without suspicion to gain strength. Considerations of diligence in our work, success in our profession, making handsome provisions for our children tend to cloud our better judgments. In our few breaks for leisure, our exhausted spirits need refreshment. The serious matter of our immortal souls is speculative and too grave and gloomy to answer the purpose, so we fly to something better deserving the name of relaxation until we are once more called back to the daily round of labour.

Meanwhile religion scarcely enters our thoughts and when we start to experience some secret misgivings, company soon drowns, amusements dissipate, or our regular occupations displace or smother our rising apprehension. Professional and commercial men often quiet their consciences by the plea that their business leaves them with no time at present to think on these serious subjects. 'Men of leisure they admit should consider them; they themselves will so do later when they retire, but meanwhile they are usefully or at least innocently employed.' Thus business and pleasure fill our time, and the 'one thing needful' is forgotten. Respected by others, and secretly applauding ourselves, maybe congratulating ourselves that we are not like such a one who is a spendthrift or a mere man of pleasure, or a notorious miser, the true principle of action is no less lacking in us, and personal advancement or the acquisition of wealth dominates our horizon.

So it is that the heart's supreme desires are permitted quite uncontrolled to take the course which best suits our temperament or to which our various situations and circumstances direct them.

But God desires to be enthroned in man's heart and to reign there without rival. If He is excluded from His rightful place for whatever reason, be it greed, sensuality, sloth, ambition, vanity and self-love, or the desire of literary fame or of military glory, we are alike estranged from the rule of the one who is our rightful sovereign. Do not let this appear to be the position; it can only do so if reference is not made to what was shown to be the essential nature of true religion. He who bowed to the god of medicine or of eloquence, was no less an idolater than he who worshipped lewdness or theft. In the various examples which have been given, the acts themselves are different, but the principle of disaffection is the same. We must prepare ourselves to meet the punishment reserved for rebels on that tremendous day when there will no longer be any room for evasions or smooth plausibilities. Learn that, 'What is highly valued among men is detestable in God's sight' (Luke 16:15).

These fundamental truths seem to have vanished from the mind and, as a result, things are seen less and less from a religious standpoint. Idleness, thoughtlessness, dissipation, the misapplication of time or of talents, the trifling away of life in frivolous occupations or unprofitable studies, all of these things we may regret in those around us, because of the effects they have on their lives. But they are not considered in a religious connection, or seen as a danger to everlasting happiness. Excessive vanity and ambition are spoken of as weaknesses rather than as sins. Even covetousness, though hateful, if not extreme, is hardly seen as against religion. We enquire solicitously after a sick or injured friend, we visit him, perhaps we regret that he does not receive better advice, and how we should reproach ourselves, if we were to neglect to do anything in our power which would contribute to his recovery! But we have no solicitude for his spiritual interest. Here he is treated just like the unfortunate traveller in the Gospel. We look at him. We can see only too well his sad condition, but (priest and Levite alike) we pass by on the other side, and leave him to the good mercies of some poor despised Samaritan.

Take the case of our children. We are deeply concerned for their happiness which should be determined on right principles. Yet in their education and marriage, the choice of their professions, consideration and judgment of the different aspects of their differing characters, how little do we take account of the fact that they are immortal beings! Health, learning, credit, the lovable and agreeable qualities and, above all, fortune and success in life, are all taken into account. Sadly, little thought is given to the probable effect which our plans for them have on their eternal interests! Such are the fatal and widespread effects which follow from the commission of the fundamental error of not considering religion to be a principle of universal application. Thus emasculated, religion now takes the form of a cold compilation of restraints and prohibitions, and the content of these is not particularly palatable. Furthermore, everyone where his own cause is involved will be likely to construe them in his own favour. Sometimes it is the words rather than the spirit of Scripture's injunctions that we fix on, overlooking the principle involved which a better acquaintance with God's word would have taught us clearly to infer. At other times, the spirit of an injunction is all; that we regard and this we do so cleverly as to obliterate or considerably ease the strictness of the terms. It is said 'What is not expressly forbidden cannot be very wrong, whatever is not emphatically urged, cannot be absolutely necessary.' If we do not actually break laws, what more can be expected from us? The people to whom the Gospel's strict precepts were given, were in very different circumstances from those in which we find ourselves. The injunctions were drawn rather tighter than is really necessary in order to allow for a little relaxation in practice. The expressions used by the writers in Scripture are figurative; the eastern style is full of hyperbole!

By these and other such dishonest twists, which rarely deceive anyone, the pure, strong morality of God's word is explained away, and its rigid canons are eased in much the same way as people argue themselves out of the obligations of human laws by similar logic.

But when the law, both in spirit and letter, is inflexible then what we cannot bend to our purpose we must break. We hear excuses like this. 'We hope our sins are of the smaller kind: harmless gallantry, innocent jollity, a few foolish expletives which we use from the mere force of habit, meaning nothing by them; a little licence of expression, a few liberties of speech in the gaiety of our hearts, which, though not perhaps strictly true, only the over-rigid would record them as more than pardonable. Even grave and religious men may indulge in this way when they relax. We serve one who is all-merciful who knows how frail we are, the number and strength of our temptations, and will not be too hard on our mistakes. We hope we are not worse than the average. All are imperfect. We admit that we have our weaknesses, we wish we were better, and trust as we grow older we shall become so. We acknowledge that our admission to a state of future happiness is due not to our own merit but to God's clemency and our Redeemer's mercy.'

But do not mistake this language for that of true Christian humility, of which its essence is to feel the burden of sin, and to long for release. The people we have been speaking about amuse themselves unconcernedly on sin's very borders, and actually dally with it with easy familiarity in its less offensive forms and thus indicate that they have no aversion to it. No love of holiness is to be seen or any attempt to acquire it; they make no effort to prepare their souls to receive God's Spirit or to expel or control those things likely to bar His entrance, or dispute His sovereignty.

It is to be deplored that the result of regarding religion merely as a collection of laws, and not as a principle within the individual, is that it soon comes to be regarded as a form of behaviour rather than a state of mind. To maintain that the practice is more vital than the internal principles from which the practice flows, is about as reasonable as the architect who saves money by economising in laying foundations, from an idea that the money could be more usefully spent on the superstructure. We know what would be the fate of such a building.

While it is true that all pretence at internal principles of holiness is vain, when conduct contradicts it, it is no less sure that the only effective way to improve our conduct is by attending vigilantly to the former. Our Saviour commented, 'Make a tree good and its fruit will be good' (Matt. 12:33), and Scripture abounds with warnings to make the cultivation of our hearts our diligent, impartial and continuous care. For it is the heart which constitutes a man and his behaviour derives its whole character and meaning from the inner motives and disposition.

Although this is such an obvious truth that it may seem almost needless to have mentioned it, it is a truth which we are apt to lose sight of in the context of our spiritual lives. It is directly opposed to the practice of considering religion as consisting of behaviour patterns rather than internal principles.

Wherever such a viewpoint is held, then trouble in some form will result. Evil feelings like poisonous weeds appear and grow with ease; while the graces of a Christian disposition, which grow tenderly in the human heart, like some of the more tender plants in the garden, require our constant assiduous care. But far from seeking them earnestly or rearing them watchfully with constant prayers for the divine grace so necessary for success, the holders of this viewpoint make no attempt to grow such 'plants', or else they are permitted to droop and die without any effort to preserve them. This leaves the way clear for other characteristics to appear and grow unhindered. Directly opposed to the Christian graces these spread and quietly take over the mind.

Some of the most important areas of the Christian

disposition in which most nominal Christians appear to be deficient have been commented upon already in this and in the preceding chapter. Many others, however, need to be isolated.

First, it is an overall characteristic of true Christians that they 'live by faith, not by sight' (2 Cor. 5:7). This means that they believe so firmly in the doctrine of future rewards and punishments as to be induced to adhere to the path of duty even though tempted by present interests and gratification to forsake it. Furthermore, the ideas uppermost in their minds and in which they are most interested are the truths revealed in Scripture. Such a state of mind helps to gain a true perspective and to bring a nearer view of those eternal things which, because of their remoteness, are either overlooked or appear but faintly on the distant horizon. The objects of this present life which fill the human eye and assume a false magnitude from their vicinity are instead seen in their proper perspective. The true Christian knows from experience, however, that the former view tends very easily to fade from sight, while the latter tends to fill his vision. His continual concern must be to preserve that right balance of views, which God in His mercy has given him. Not that he should withdraw from that position in life which Providence has provided, but rather he will be active in life's business and enjoy its comforts with self-control and a thankful heart. He will not however give up his whole being to them, but will keep them subordinate in his concern to objects of greater importance.

For him 'what is seen is temporary, but what is unseen is eternal' (2 Cor. 4:18) and in life's tumult and bustle he is sobered by the still small voice which whispers to him, 'this world in its present form is passing away' (1 Cor. 7:31). This alone must give him an entirely different outlook from that of the average nominal Christian who is almost entirely taken up with present-day concerns. They know that they are mortal, but they do not feel it. They have the truth in their understandings, but not in their hearts. How different from those who recognise the infinite importance of eternal things, and with it have an awareness of the shortness and uncertainty of this life. A conviction that, 'Night is coming when no-one can work' (John 9:4) produces a firmness of spirit which hardens us against fortune's buffets and keeps us from being too deeply absorbed in the cares, interests, goods or evils of this transitory life. So a right view of the relative value of temporal and eternal things maintains the soul in a state of calm composure whatever life's vicissitudes. It both quickens our diligence and moderates our ardour. It encourages right pursuits, yet checks any undue concern regarding their success and thus enables us to 'use the things of the world, as if not engrossed in them' (1 Cor. 7:31).

But there are other distinctions to be found between nominal and real Christians. There are numerous injunctions in Scripture which indicate how a Christian should live and behave. For the nominal Christian these have no great attraction and certainly they would not be regarded as a source of pleasure. But this is the light in which a true Christian regards them. He walks as a Christian, not by constraint, but willingly. It is a safe and comfortable path. Not that he is not aware of the necessity of both constant support and watchfulness with which his former values and affections are apt to reassert themselves. Earnest prayers for God's help must be offered and every effort made to exert self-control so that things likely to cloud his judgment are avoided. It becomes his unwearied endeavour to grow in the knowledge and appreciation of the things of heaven.

In Scripture we find Christians represented as setting their affections on higher things, as rejoicing in God's service and delighting in His worship. But for most nominal Christians pleasure and religion are contradictory terms. They may look with something of secret satisfaction on their religious practices, and even experience it during their performance because they are engaged in the discharge of a duty. But this is entirely different from the pleasure which derives from an activity which in itself is agreeable to us. Does the service and worship of God give pleasure to these people? Do they give rise to feelings of calm composure and thankfulness which bespeaks a mind at peace with itself and those around? Is it engaged in a service which is to its taste and feelings?

Take Sunday as one example. Do they gladly avail themselves of the opportunity to withdraw from business and other cares? Is the day spent cheerfully in the way that was intended? Do they go to church, and when not there how do they spend their time? Are they busy studying God's word, pondering His perfections, admiring His handiwork, reviewing His redeeming love and in singing His praises? When they are alone is it for earnest thanksgiving, self-examination and intercession? If they have the right talents or wealth, do they spend part of this day of leisure in helping the needy, visiting the sick, comforting the sorrowful, in planning the good of their fellows or in considering how they may best further the temporal and spiritual interests of their friends and acquaintances? Or if theirs is a larger sphere of influence do they plan ways whereby with God's help, they may be used more extensively in the spread of the Gospel? When relaxing with family and friends does their conversation reveal the subject which fills their hearts? Does their speech and manner show them to be unusually gentle, kind, friendly and devoid of irritating behaviour and habits?

Surely a whole day does not seem long when spent in this way. The proper uses of a Christian Sabbath have been pointed out, not only because the day spent in this way is conducive, under God, to the maintenance of spiritual health, but also because we must all have noted that many decent and respectable people seem to be destitute of religious resources. Sunday for them is at best a heavy day and the larger part of it, which is not taken up with attendance at church, drags dully on in a comfortless emptiness. This is not to mention those who by their more open profaning of this holy day violate the laws and insult the religion of their country. How little do they seem to enter into the spirit of Christian belief, while not disregarding entirely its external behaviour. They plead strongly against being forced to spend the whole of the day devoted to religion, claiming considerable merit for giving up a part of it believing that this gives them the right to spend the remainder as they choose. How cleverly they seize upon any plausible excuse for performing some week-day activity on Sunday, while not showing the same propensity to introduce any of Sunday's special activities into the rest of the week! They find excuses for taking journeys, writing letters, balancing accounts; in short doing anything, which with a little forethought could probably have been anticipated, or, without great inconvenience, postponed!

Even business is recreation, compared with religion, and from the drudgery of this sacred day of rest they fly for relief to their ordinary occupations. There are others who would consider business or playing cards as profaning the Sabbath, yet find the day drags and seek relief in social or family visits where there is no pretence that their conversation turns to such topics as might be conducive to religious instruction or improvement. Meanwhile their families are neglected, their servants deprived of Christian privileges, and their example noted by others who cannot see that they themselves are any less religiously employed while playing an innocent game of cards or going to a concert.

All these different devices, whatever they may be, to unhallow Sunday and change its character, prove only too clearly that our worship of God is by constraint and not a willing service, which we are glad, therefore, to curtail though we dare not omit it altogether.

There are those who will confess with concern and sadness that this is the situation in which they find themselves. They pray humbly and endeavour diligently to be less readily distracted in their times of devotion and for a heart more open to appreciate spiritual things. They care to guard against whatever tends to anchor their affections to earthly enjoyments. Do not let these people be discouraged. We are not condemning them, but they are those who accept the Christian way yet proceed in the opposite direction. They do not seem to realise that there is anything wrong with them. They voluntarily fall in with a state of mind directly contrary to God's positive commands which is in direct contrast to the way that Scripture pictures the Christian character, and accords only too well with the character of those whom Scripture states to be the objects of divine displeasure and ultimate punishment.

However, it is not only in these essential devotional constituents that most nominal Christians are defective. This, they freely admit with some secret complacency at their frankness, is a higher strain of piety than that to which they aspire. Their forgetfulness also of some of the leading aspects of Christian behaviour is obvious from their lack in showing kindness, meekness, gentleness, patience, long-suffering and, above all, that humility and lowliness of mind which perhaps more than in any other quality char- acterises Christian behaviour. These temperamental fea- tures are not only neglected, but even repudiated and exploded, while their opposites are acknowledged and applauded. A just pride, a proper and suitable pride, are terms we hear regularly. To possess a high spirit, to behave with proper spirit when ill-used – by which is meant a quickness at taking offence and a promptness in showing resentment – is commended; while a meekness so com- mended by Scripture calls forth disapproval and contempt. Vanity and vain-glory are allowed free rein in the heart. But this is a topic of such importance, and on which so many mistakes have been written and said, that it demands a separate section.

Section III
On the desire of human estimation and applause. The generally prevailing opinions contrasted with those of the true Christian

The desire to be held higher in the estimation of others, to be honoured, admired and praised by our fellows is the most common of all passions. While perhaps more con- spicuous in the upper classes, it spares neither age, sex, nor status. It appears in various guises or may remain hidden while influencing what we think, speak and do. Sometimes it is the main pursuit in life and the driving principle. But where this is not the case, in the society beauty, the author, no less than in the soldier, it is often the soul's master passion.

Parents joyfully recognise this principle in their infants. It is diligently instilled and nurtured, as years advance, under the names of honourable ambition and praiseworthy imitation. Schools and colleges aim to excite and foster it. The writer is well aware that he will be thought in attacking this form of behaviour to be pushing his opinions too far. It will be argued that to remove this principle would be like taking from the world the principle of motion, without which all would be torpid, cold and comfortless. It might also be observed, 'We should not deviate from the paths of duty in order to ensure man's approval or to avoid his reproaches. We accept that the love of praise is sometimes a ridiculous, or mischievous passion to which we owe coquetry, conceit and the noxious race of heroes and conquerors. We also are prepared, when it appears in the shape of vanity, to test it as a foible, or in that of false glory, to condemn it as a crime. But all these are only its perversions and to contend just because of these that the principle is wrong leads to the error of arguing against the use of a healthy principle altogether, simply because it is liable to occasional abuse. When properly applied it gives rise to every dignified and generous undertaking. It forces indolence into activity, and extorts generosity and virtue from vice itself. The soul, once warmed by its generous ardour, no difficulties deter, no dangers terrify and no labours tire.'

All this and much more might be argued by the advocates of this particular viewpoint. It would not be difficult to show that such a eulogy is unmerited. Quite apart from the argument based on the idea of the innocence of error, the principle is as manifestly inconstant and variable as there are types of fashion, habit and opinion in different periods and societies. What it tolerates in one age, it forbids in another. What it prescribes and applauds in one country, in another it condemns and stigmatises! It blatantly praises evil and denounces virtue. It is calculated to produce the appearance rather than the reality of excellence, and at best not to check the love of evil but only its commission. Much of this indeed was seen and acknowledged by the philosophers and poets of the pagan world. They declaimed it as a principle both mutable and inconsistent. They lamented its fatal effects which, under the name of false glory, it had produced on man's peace and happiness. They condemned the pursuit when it led its followers from the path of virtue, and taught that only the praise of the wise and good was to be desired.

But it was left to Scripture to point out clearly the defect and viciousness of this view and to reveal to us more fully its encroaching character and dangerous tendencies. It also teaches us how it may be purified from its corrupting qualities, reduced and subordinated and used legitimately, and directed to its proper end.

The Bible repeatedly reminds us that God formed us originally and that we are continually dependent on His generosity. We also learn the painful lesson of man's degradation and unworthiness, that humiliation and contrition are the state of mind best suited to our fallen condition and most acceptable to our Creator. We read that we should make it our practice to cherish and cultivate this state of mind (to the repression and extinction of the spirit of arrogance and self-importance, which is so natural to man's heart). Any natural advantages which we may possess over others, any moral superiority, for all these we are wholly indebted to God's unmerited goodness. The great end and purpose of all revelation is to reclaim us from our natural pride and selfishness with their fatal consequences and to bring us to a true sense of our weakness and depravity, so that with unfeigned humility we fall down and glorify God. '. . . no-one may boast before him. Let him who boasts boast in the Lord' (1 Cor. 1:29, 31). 'The eyes of the arrogant man will be humbled and the pride of men brought low; the Lord alone will be exalted' (Isa. 2:11).

Sadly these solemn admonitions are too often disregarded and their relationship to this subject entirely overlooked, even by Christian moralists. These authors do not refer to the source and internal principle of conduct, but speak of the love of human applause as meritorious or culpable, as the desire of true or false glory, according to the effect that it produces in the individual to mankind in general. But it is clearly the judgment of the word of God that the love of worldly admiration and applause is in its nature thoroughly corrupt. The reason is that it is self-glorifying instead of ascribing all the honour and glory where only they are due. Its guilt, therefore, is not to be measured by its effects on man's happiness, nor is it to be classed as true or false glory, depending on the ends to which it is directed, beneficial or mischievous, just or unjust, but it is false because it exalts that which ought to be put down and criminal, because it encroaches on God's prerogative.

The Scriptures, in addition, teach that not only is man prone to err, so that sometimes the world's commendations may be mistaken, but also having a warped judgment and a depraved heart, its applauses and contempt will largely be misplaced. It also teaches that while the beneficent and disinterested spirit of Christianity, with its capacity to promote domestic comfort and general happiness is praise-worthy; yet an aspiring after more than ordinary excellence gives rise to secret misgivings in others, or a sense of inferiority mixed with envy, leading to offence. God's word teaches that though these Christian doctrines and precepts which do conflict with worldly interests, pursuits, principles and systems, may be professed without offence, yet those which oppose or are different from them will be seen as needlessly precise and strict, the outcome of a morose and gloomy spirit, the marks of a mean, enslaved, or distorted understanding. The follower of Christ on this account must be prepared to forgo worldly favour from time to time. Let him beware also when the world bestows its favour lavishly.

Since our desires should be upon heavenly things and objects and since, in particular, God's love and favour ought to be our supreme and regular desire, to which all else is subordinated, it follows that the love of human applause must be injurious since it tends to confine and circumscribe our desires to the narrow limits of this world. Its special snare is that it disposes us to estimate too highly, and love too well, man's good opinion and commendation.

But though Scripture warns us against the desire and pursuit of worldly estimation and honour, it reduces their value and prepares us to lose or relinquish them if need be, it also teaches us that Christians are not only not called upon absolutely and voluntarily to renounce or forgo them, but that when unsought they are bestowed on us for actions intrinsically good, we are to accept that as part of God's Providence. We ought to pay due respect and regard to the approval and favour of men, but not value these simply for our own gratification, but as providing a means of influence which can be turned to good account by diverting them to the improvement and happiness of our fellow-men and glorifying God.

Credit and reputation are, in the eyes of the Christian, akin to riches. He will neither prize nor desire and pursue them, but if they are allotted to him by the hand of Providence he will accept them thankfully and use them with moderation. He will relinquish them when it is necessary, without a murmur. He will guard himself against all greed and selfishness, which they are too apt to produce and foster. While in themselves acceptable because of the weakness of his nature, they are highly dangerous possessions to be valued, not as a means to luxury or splendour, but as a way to bring honour to his Saviour and to alleviate some of man's miseries.

It is not the way of Christianity to extinguish natural desires, but to bring them under proper control, and to direct them to their true objectives. The command is not to set our hearts on earthly treasures, but to remember that we have in heaven 'better and lasting possessions' (Heb. 10:34) than this world can bestow. While repressing our concern for earthly credit, and moderating our attachment to it, Christian belief sets before us and urges us to aspire after the splendours of that better state of true glory, honour and immortality. This is a justifiable ambition, suited to our high calling and worthy of our energies which would never be satisfied by the transient distinctions of this life.

There can be no doubt that the light in which worldly credit and esteem are regarded by most professing Christians is extremely different from that in which they are placed by Scripture. The inordinate love of worldly glory implies a passion which from the nature of things cannot be exercised by most people. The right sort of situation rarely presents itself. But everywhere we discover the same principle in a lesser shape or form applicable to common life. We may discover it in an excessive love of distinction, admiration and praise, in the universal acceptableness of flattery and, above all, in the excessive value that we put on worldly character. It is guarded with watchfulness. Questioning causes jealousy, attack brings resentments. Its loss leads to bitterness and suffering. All these emotions are too real to be disputed or denied. Dishonour, disgrace and shame present a picture of horror too dreadful to be faced.

The consequences of all this are natural and obvious. Worldly credit is held to be of the highest intrinsic worth and worldly shame as the greatest of all possible evils. We sometimes juggle with the path of duty so as to favour our obtaining the one, and avoidance of the other. When this cannot be done, we boldly and openly turn aside from that path, declaring the temptation to be too strong to resist.

Numerous proofs of the truth of these assertions can readily be produced. It is shown, for instance, by that general tendency of religion to conceal herself from view, though by no means altogether extinct, she is apt to vanish from our conversations and to be replaced by pretended licentiousness of sentiment and behaviour and a false show of unbelief. It is shown by that tendency to comply, acquiesce and participate in the habits and manners of this dissipated age, which almost obliterates any external distinction between the Christian and the unbeliever. It has made it very rare to find anyone who dares to be known as a Christian oddity, or who can say with the apostle, 'I am not ashamed of the gospel' (Rom. 1:16). It is shown by that quick resentment, those bitter disputes, those angry retorts, those malicious triumphs, that impatience of inferiority, that awareness of past defeats, and promptness to revenge them, which too often change the character of a Christian debating chamber into that of a ring for prize-fighters. The proprieties of public conduct and the rules of social decorum are violated while all the charities propounded by Jesus are renounced and excluded.

But from all lesser proofs, our attention is drawn to one of a still larger size, the practice of duelling. This is a practice which, to the disgrace of a Christian society, has long been allowed to exist with little restraint or opposition. Its basis rests mainly on that excessive overvaluation of character, which teaches that worldly credit is to be preserved at all costs, and disgrace must be avoided. The unreasonableness of duelling has often been proved and on various principles it has been shown to be criminal. But its essential guilt has almost escaped notice, that is that there is a deliberate preference of man's favour before God's at a moment when our own life and that of a fellow-creature are at stake, and we run the risk of rushing into the presence of our Maker in the very act of causing Him offence. It would take too long to enumerate the evils which spring from the practice. But there is one observation which has been too often overlooked. In the judgment of a religion which requires a pure heart, and of the one to whom 'thought is action', he cannot be held to be innocent if he lives with settled determination to commit a particular crime when the opportunity presents itself. This consideration places duelling on quite a different footing from almost any other crime.

It is to be hoped that these observations on the love of worldly estimation have been sufficient to make it evident that this principle is of a highly questionable nature. Rather it should be brought into subjection and carefully guarded. If sometimes it stimulates great and generous undertakings, if it encourages hard work and even excellence, if in a more limited sphere it produces courtesy and kindness, we must yet remember the ambition which lays waste nations, and the competitiveness and resentments which interrupt society's harmony. The former has indeed been acknowledged, but the latter have been given insufficient attention. Its poisonous effect on the basic and distinguishing graces of Christian behaviour has not been pointed out.

To read the writings of some Christian moralists and to note how little they seem disposed to question the matter except where a raving conqueror is involved, one is tempted to suspect that since it is such a widespread and potent principle they despair of ever subjecting it. Rather they endeavour to compliment it into a good humour, like barbarous nations which worship evil spirits because of fear.

But the truth is that the reasonings of Christian moralists too often show scant evidence of genuine Christian morality. The case before us is an example of this. This principle of the desire for worldly distinction and praise is often too easily permitted and even commended. It is base and sordid to covet wealth, yet to covet honour is treated as indicating a generous and worthy nature. These writers seem to forget that while the principle in question tends to prevent the commission of those grosser acts of evil which would be harmful to our reputation, it not only stops there, but then begins to exert almost an equal force in the opposite direction. They do not consider that this principle is liable, even in the case of those who move in a limited sphere, to fill us with empty vanities and evil desires. Above all, it tends to fix the feelings on earthly things and to steal the heart away from God. They admit that it is criminal when it produces harmful effects, but forget how apt it is by substituting a false and corrupt motive, to vitiate our good actions, depriving them of all that made them of value.

The distinguishing feature of Christians is that they are not satisfied with superficial appearances, but wish to rectify their motives and purify their hearts. The true Christian, in obedience to Scripture, is nowhere more on guard than where the desire of human estimation and distinction is in question. At no other time does he feel more deeply his own weakness or seek and pray more diligently for divine assistance. He may watch and pray against a passion's encroachments which when permitted to go beyond its rightful limits reveal a peculiar hostility to the graces which distinguish the Christian disposition. This passion will unconsciously become stronger because it is in continual use and almost everything else feeds it. In consequence, its growth is favoured and cherished, helped on by pride and selfishness, the natural and perhaps inexterminable inhabitants of the human heart.

Being made aware of the importance of guarding against the progress of this encroaching principle, and relying humbly on help from above, the pure Christian thankfully makes use of the means, considerations and motives suggested to him for that purpose by the word of God. He spends time in turning out his weaknesses. He endeavours to gain and maintain a right conviction of his great unworthiness and always to remember that whatever distinguishes him from others is not properly his own, but that he owes it to the undeserved bounty of heaven. He tries diligently to keep a proper sense of the true value of human distinction and applause, knowing that he will covet them the less as he learns not to overrate their value. He remembers, too, how undeserved they often are and how precarious. The disapproval of good men rightly causes him to suspect himself, and prompts him to examine carefully and impartially those parts of his character, or conduct, which have drawn on him the criticism. The favourable opinion and praises of good men are rightly acceptable to him. But even when commended he does not allow himself to be led astray by overvaluing this, lest he should come to substitute it for his conscience. He guards against this danger by remembering how indistinctly we can discern each other's motives, or enter into each other's circumstances, and how mistaken, therefore, may be the judgments formed of us and our actions, even by good men. It is not improbable that at some time we may be compelled to forfeit their esteem, by adhering to the dictates of our own consciences.

But if he tries to sit loosely to favour and applause, even from good men since he is aware of their worth as means and instruments of usefulness and influence under the limitations and for the ends permitted in Scripture, he is observant to acquire, will be glad to possess and careful to retain them. He will regard them, however, as desirable, not simply to possess but also to use. He will hold himself responsible for the share of them which he enjoys, and be bound both not to let them lie unemployed and not to lavish them.

Acting on these principles, he will carefully use what worldly credit he enjoys to remove or lessen any prejudices in conciliation, and by these means make way for the progress of truth. He will make it his business to initiate and encourage charitable and useful schemes. Where these require a united effort he will try to obtain and preserve such co-operation. But while striving to keep his reputation (so long as he has one) subservient to the advance of religion and virtue, and promoting the happiness and comfort of his fellows, he will not transgress Scripture's precepts just in order to obtain, cultivate or preserve it. He will resolutely disclaim the fallacious reasoning of 'doing evil that good may come'.

While prepared to relinquish his reputation when necessary, he will not cast it away. Insofar as he is permitted he will avoid occasions of diminishing it, instead of studiously seeking or multiplying them as is the habit of some worthy but imprudent men. If his reputation is sacrificed at all, it will be at the call of duty and not because of ill behaviour, bad language or other misdemeanours. The world will agree that he is both amiable and respectable; though with regard to religion, they may consider him unreasonably precise and strict. His aim will be to leave the enemies of religion with only the confession of Daniel's accusers, who said, 'We will never find any basis for charges against this man Daniel unless it has something to do with the law of his God' (Dan. 6:5), and if he falls into disfavour, it will not be because of any dishonourable conduct, but because of the false standards of a misjudging world. If such a misunderstanding arises he will not withdraw himself from society, but will be ready to clear up any doubts, to explain what has been only partly known and 'speaking the truth in love' (Eph. 4:15) to correct erroneous impressions.

Sometimes he may feel it his duty to vindicate his character publicly from unjust reproach, and to repel false charges, but he will guard carefully against pride leading him away or being turned into some untruth or lack of Christian charity, when treading such a dangerous path. At such a time he must not be unduly concerned about his worldly reputation for its own sake, and when he has done what duty requires for its vindication, it will not concern him unduly if his efforts have been to no avail. In every age and nation good men have frequently been unjustly slandered and disgraced. If in such circumstances, even in pagan darkness, they have been consoled by a clean conscience, shall one who is cheered by the Christian's hope and assured that a day will shortly come where all secrets will be revealed, including the mistaken judgments of men, perhaps even of good men, which will be corrected and that 'each will receive his praise from God' (1 Cor. 4:5), shall such a one give up or even bend or droop under such a trial?

There might be more excuse for the overvaluing of human reputation by those for whom the other side of the grave is dark and cheerless. They might also be pardoned for pursuing the glory which might survive them, seeking thereby to extend the narrow span of their earthly existence. But how different for the Christian for whom these clouds are rolled away, and for whom 'Christ Jesus . . . has brought life and immortality to light through the gospel' (2 Tim. 1:10). Worldly favour and distinction are among the best things this world has to offer, but the Christian knows that the condition of his calling is that his portion is not here. As in the case of any earthly enjoyments, so with worldly honour he dreads, lest his highest feelings being satisfied by these, it should later be said to him, '. . . remember that in your lifetime you received your good things' (Luke 16:25).

His holy calling requires him to be victorious over the world, combining this with a conquest of the fear of its disesteem and dishonour. He reflects on the lives of those holy men who 'faced jeers and flogging' (Heb. 11:36); and remembers that our Saviour was Himself 'despised and rejected by men' (Isa. 53:3). What is he this Christian, that he should be exempt from the common lot, or consider it's too much to bear the malicious gossip accorded to his profession?

But he finds that the most effective way to get into a proper frame of mind regarding the love of human approbation is to cultivate the issue 'to obtain the praise that comes from the only God' (John 5:44). Christian, would you really bring this feeling under proper control? If so, then lift up your heart and thoughts until the praises and the censures of men fade away and the still, small voice of conscience is no longer drowned by the noises of the world below. Our vision here is liable to be taken up with earthly things and our hearing engrossed with earthly sounds. There you will glimpse that dazzling and incorruptible crown which is held out to you in the realms of light, and your ears will be delighted by a heavenly melody! Here we are in a variable atmosphere – the outlook darkened at one time by the gloom of disgrace, and at another it is dazzling with the gleamings of glory. But now you have ascended above this changeable region and no storms disturb or clouds obscure the air while the lightning plays and the thunder rolls beneath you.

In this way the Christian from time to time exercises himself and when he descends from this elevated region to the plain below, and mixes in the bustle of life, he still retains the memories of his time of withdrawal. By this means the unseen world becomes a reality to him and he makes it a habit to speak and act as in the presence of 'thousands upon thousands of angels in joyful assembly, to the church of the first born, whose names are written in heaven. You have come to God the judge of all' (Heb. 12:22–3). The consciousness of their approval cheers and gladdens his soul in the face of the scoffs and reproaches of a misjudging world, and their united praises form a harmony uninterrupted by a few discordant earthly voices.

But because the Christian is sometimes enabled to triumph over the excessive love of human praise, he does not then regard himself as safe from its intrusion. On the contrary, he is conscious that the temptation is so strong that even where it seems under control, if circumstances are favourable it will spring up again with renewed vigour. The Christian is aware that he is particularly vulnerable in those areas where he excels. There is a danger that his pure motives become unconsciously corrupted as he becomes anxious about worldly favour. It can happen in his attempting to make his goodness attractive to and respected by others, and true to Scripture's teaching, to let his 'light shine before men, that they may see your good deeds and praise your Father in heaven' (Matt. 5:16).

He keeps a watch on himself both on small and great occasions. The latter in the case of most people rarely occur, whereas the former repeatedly arise and so they can serve a very useful purpose in helping to form and strengthen a right mental attitude in the circumstances in question. They are the means most readily available whereby we may find out our true character. Do not miss these opportunities. If anyone finds himself shrinking from disfavour over small matters while consoling himself that if the need arose he could deal with a more vigorous trial, then let him think again. Let him reflect that these small matters, where no credit is to be gained and little self-satisfaction is to be found even by the vainest, provide the test of whether or not we are ashamed of the Gospel of Christ, and willing for the best of reasons to bear reproach for the name of Jesus.

The Christian also knows that an excessive desire to gain human approval is a very subtle emotion which can spread universally. It can lurk unseen or under most specious disguises, so that it insinuates itself into his very religion. Arrogant devotion and pretentious charity with other over-manifestations appear. These have often been condemned and we can without difficulty discover the tendencies towards them in ourselves. The Christian should not allow himself to be deceived by any outward differences between himself and the world, but he should beware lest, as a result of the unconscious invasion by this subtle emotion referred to, his religion should come to have only 'a reputation of being alive' (Rev. 3:1). If this is not the case then he should closely examine his motives, lest he be prompted to extra-ordinary religious observances, and the avoidance of lewd behaviour, not so much by his strict standards of holiness as by a fear of losing the good opinion of his stricter associates, or even of falling in the estimation of the world at large. Those who wish to conform to the admonitions of God's word need to be watchful and keep a close and frequent scrutiny of their own hearts, so that they will not find out too late that they have been mistaken as to what are their true motives.

Let them, above all, pray humbly and earnestly for God's help to fix in their beings a deep, continual and practical awareness of the excellence of God-given honour and of the comparative worthlessness of all earthly esteem and pre-eminence. Unless the soul's feelings are predomi-nantly occupied with achieving heavenly rather than human honour, even though we may have relinquished the pursuit of fame, we shall not have acquired the state of mind which can bear disgrace and shame. There is a wide gap between these two states and the one who believes he has arrived at the one, must not therefore conclude he has reached the other. The one may be gained simply by a little natural moderation and an even temper. The other, however, we can attain slowly and with much discipline.

The Christian's disregard of human praise should not result in a life of neglect and indolence. His behaviour should always warrant praise and fame, although he does not seek it. It should be apparent that it is not the need of worldly approval that spurs him on, but something infinitely superior. This will be evident not only in his moral uprightness but also in his love and humility.

Humility, by reducing our own value of ourselves, should moderate our claims on worldly esteem. Our tendency to ostentation and display will be checked, prompting us to avoid rather than attract attention. It will dispose us to sit down in quiet obscurity, even though we believe ourselves to be better entitled to the credit that has been conferred on others.

The disposition of a Christian is not one of sordid sensuality, lazy apathy, pride, or disappointed ambition, but it is a mixture of firmness, tranquillity, peace and love. It manifests itself in acts of kindness and courtesy. Popularity and unpopularity do not change it. So it remains unshaken in its constancy, unwearied in its benevolence, firm without being rough and assiduous without being servile.

Section IV
The generally prevailing error, of substituting amiable tempers and useful lives in the place of religion, stated and confuted; with hints to real Christians

There is another practical error which is very prevalent. Its effects are highly injurious to the cause of religion. The error is that of exaggerating the merit of certain attractive and useful qualities in an individual's character and of considering them sufficient to compensate for the lack of a love and fear of God.

It seems to be a very prevalent opinion that kindness and a sweet temper, sympathising, benevolent, generous emotions, attention to domestic, relative and social duties, and above all, a life of general activity and usefulness, make up for the lack of what is termed religion.

Many will declare that the difference between the qualities mentioned and religion is verbal rather than real; for in truth, are they not religion in substance, if not in name? Is it not the objective of religion and in particular the glory of Christianity to extinguish evil outbursts, to curb violence, to control appetites and to smooth man's roughness to make us compassionate and forgiving of one another. It also makes us good husbands, good fathers, good friends and active and useful in the discharge of our duties.

So a fatal distinction is drawn between morality and religion. It is a great and serious error, which it is very important to notice because many who would condemn the language in which this opinion is expressed as too strong are tainted to some degree by the same idea. Under its almost beguiling influence they are vainly comforting their imagination and repressing their well-grounded fears about their own spiritual state. They are also quieting their justifiable concerns for the spiritual welfare of others, and soothing themselves regarding their own neglect of making attempts to help the others.

Their cursory and superficial views emphasise how easily men satisfy themselves in religious matters. Their untruths and fallacies must be acknowledged by anyone who accepts the authority of Scripture. Even judged by a lesser standard, it is not difficult to show that the moral value of these sweet and kindly dispositions and useful lives is much overrated. These people obtain our favour and disarm our judgments by their genial and apparently disinterested behaviour. They prompt men to flatter rather than to humiliate us, to sympathise with our joys or sorrows and they excel in their attentiveness and courtesy, and by their obvious tendency to produce and maintain harmonious relations socially and at home. It is not unworthy, however, to remark that there are many who pretend to have these desirable attributes and thereby gain undeserved credit. It is an assumed character worn in public, the better to conceal quite the opposite temperaments. To see this sweet, courteous man stripped of his sham covering, follow him to his home. There you will find him selfish and bad tempered, harassing and annoying the poor wretches whom he tyrannises. It is as if he were making up for the restraint which had been imposed on him in the world.

Where such kindly qualities are genuine, it would often be more appropriate to call them amiable instincts than moral virtues. Often they do not indicate any mental conflict or previous discipline, and are apt to evaporate in empty sentiments, passing sympathy and idle wishes, and fruitless pronouncements. They do not possess that strength and force of character which, heedless of difficulties and dangers, produces ready service with vigour and perseverance. Being destitute of true firmness, they often encourage those evils which they should be repressing. They may be in danger because of their soft compliant nature, of participating in what is wrong, in addition to conniving at it. From the standpoint of truth and reason, these people make bad magistrates, bad parents and bad friends. They are lacking in those very qualities which give those relationships their principal value.

When these qualities are not grounded and rooted in religion they are sickly and transient in nature, and lack that characteristic fibre which is necessary in order to put up with the rude shocks and the changeable and boorish times to which this world exposes them. It is only of Christian love of which it is the character that it 'is patient', 'is kind', 'is not easily angered', and 'it always protects, always trusts, always hopes, always perseveres' (1 Cor. 13:4–7). In the spring of youth, we are flushed with health and confidence. Hope is young and ardent, our desires are unsatisfied and there is novelty in whatever we see. We are disposed to be good-natured the more because we are pleased. Wherever we look, we see some friendly face. All nature seems to smile at us.

So the friendly dispositions of which we have been speaking spring up naturally. The soil is suitable and the climate favourable for them. They shoot forth vigorously and bloom luxuriantly. Superficially, all seems fair and flourishing and we look forward to autumn's fruits and promise ourselves an ample crop. But by and by the sun scorches, the frost nips, the winds rise, the rain falls. All our fond expectations are dashed. Our youthful efforts maybe have been successful and we become wealthy or eminent. A kind easygoing manner has resulted, as so often it does, in a youth of easygoing social dissipation and idleness. Too late the realisation overtakes us that we have wasted that time and those opportunities which cannot be recalled or recovered. We sink into disregard and obscurity. We are thrust out of notice by accident or misfortunes and are left behind by those with whom we started on equal terms.

Originally, perhaps, they had less class and fewer advantages, but nevertheless they outstripped us in the race for honour. This is the more galling, because it appears to us, with reason, to have been chiefly owing to our generous, easy, good-natured humour, which led us – without a struggle – to give place to their more lofty claims. Thus we quietly permitted them to occupy a position to which originally we had as fair a claim as they. Our awkward and futile attempts to regain that position reveal how much we lack self-knowledge and composure in our riper years, as much as when younger we were devoid of any drive. So our inferiority is the more evident, and our discontent more obvious to a hostile world, which, not unjustly, condemns and ridicules our misplaced ambition.

With advancing years the heart is no longer cheerful and placid; and if the countenance preserves its outward appearance this is no longer the honest expression of the heart. Prosperity and luxury gradually extinguish sympathy, and by inflating with pride, harden and debase the soul. In other cases shame secretly clouds, remorse begins to sting, suspicion to corrode and jealousy and envy to embitter. Disappointed hopes, unsuccessful competitions and frustrated pursuits all sour and irritate the disposition. A little personal experience of man's selfishness dampens our warmth and kindly feelings. Above all, ingratitude sickens the heart, chills and thickens goodwill's life-blood, until at last our youthful Nero, soft and sensitive, becomes a hard and cruel tyrant and our youthful Timon, gay, generous and kindly, is changed into a cold, sour, silent misanthrope.

And, as with amiable dispositions, so with what are called useful lives, it must be admitted that their intrinsic value tends to be much overrated. They often result from a disposition which is naturally bustling and active, which delights in movements, and finds its work more than repaid, either by its intrinsic pleasure or by the credit which ensues. More than this, if it is accepted that it is religion that tends in general to produce usefulness, then these irreligious men of useful lives are rather exceptions to the general rule. It must, in fact, be said that they are useless or even positively mischievous since they either fail to encourage or actively discourage the very thing which is the underlying source of usefulness in most men. Judged by their standard, it would seem that the particular good in these men is more than counterbalanced by the general evil. If, furthermore, their behaviour was brought to account, they should be charged with losing the good which might otherwise have been produced had they acted more worthily and been themselves the source of a good religious example. They are like individuals in whom some quirk of constitution permits them to defy the ordinary rules of living which most of us have to observe. However they may plead in their own defence that they do themselves no harm, but for their excesses they would probably have enjoyed better health and kept it longer, as well as turned it to better account. They disparage the laws of self-control and lead others to break them with fatal results, they themselves having broken them with impunity.

But were the qualities in question even more meritorious, and the exceptions not liable to occur, this would in no way compensate for the lack of an individual's love and fear of God and of an overwhelming desire to promote His glory. Observing one commandment, however clearly and forcibly expressed, in no way compensates for the neglect of another enjoined with equal clearness and force. In the present instance such an argument would allow men to overlook the first part of the law providing they obeyed the second. But such a compromise is not permitted. By the same token some have sought to atone for a life of evil by strict religious observances. The former type of individual pleads industry in the interests of fellow-creatures, while the latter will claim the same done for God. Such is the unequal manner in which we treat God and each other. All would rightly consider it to be false confidence on the part of a religious thief or adulterer (accepting for the sake of argument such a solecism in terms) to console himself that he has God's approval, but many will consider it hard and over-precise to suggest that God does not approve of the confessedly irreligious man who has social and domestic concerns.

It may be remarked that the writer is not being fair in his argument in that those who discharge their duties towards their fellows are performing their duties to God in fact, if not in name. But can our opponent deny that Scripture is nowhere more full, frequent, strong and unequivocal than in enjoining us to love and fear God, to worship and serve Him continually with humble and grateful hearts and always to look on Him as our benefactor, sovereign, and Father, and be full of gratitude, loyalty and respectful love? Can he deny that these positive precepts are made even clearer, and their authority more binding, by innumerable illustrations and indirect confirmations? Who in the face of these precise commands, illustrated and confirmed in this way, would dare to maintain that, knowing their purpose and the ends they were designed to produce, would in innocence put aside or break their clear obligations on the excuse that he does conform, though in a different way, to this original plan, and produce by different means the same result?

This line of arguing is one with which, to say nothing of its offensive profanity, man's heart, prone as it is to self-deception and partiality, is not fit to be trusted. Here, once again being more cautious and apprehensive about our worldly rather than our religious interests, we see clearly the fallacy of this reasoning, and we protest against it when all attempt is made to introduce it into commerce. We see clearly that it provides the means of getting rid by turns of every moral obligation. The adulterer might permit himself, with a quiet conscience, to violate his unsuspecting friend's wife whenever he could be assured that his crime would not be detected. For where would be the evil and misery the prevention of which was the real reason for prohibiting adultery? Similarly, the thief and even the murderer might find abundant room for the innocent exercise of their respective occupations, arguing from the basic reason behind the commands forbidding theft and murder. Maybe no crime exists to which this crooked morality would not furnish some convenient entry.

The arguments which have been brought forward have sufficed to disprove the pretentious qualities under consideration, even though those qualities were by nature perfect. But they are not perfect, they are radically defective and corrupt, a body without a soul. They are animated and actuated by a false principle. Christianity – in the words of a friend – is 'a religion of motives'. Christian practice only flows from Christian principles, and none other is accepted by the one who will be obeyed as well as worshipped 'in spirit and truth' (John 4:23).

Religion's enemies sometimes compare the irreligious man with a naturally sweet and amiable temperament, with the religious man who is by nature rough and severe; and from this they draw their condescensions. But this method of reasoning is surely unjust. If they would argue fairly, they should compare persons with similar natural qualities, taking several examples. They would then be forced to admit that religion does make a difference by increasing a person's kindliness and usefulness. In those rare instances of a genuine and persistent, kindly disposition and useful life occurring without any religious background, experience leads us to believe, that true religion would have rendered them even more amiable and useful.

True Christians should always remember that they are called upon loudly to make this argument clearer and these positions even less questionable. The command is everywhere to be tender, sympathetic, diligent and useful. It is the characteristic of that 'wisdom that comes from heaven' in which you are to be proficient, that it is 'pure; then peace-loving, considerate, submissive, full of mercy and good fruit' (Jas. 3:17). The efficacy of Christian belief in softening the heart was undeniable in the sense of the apostle, Paul. It was able to transform a bigoted, furious and cruel persecutor into an almost unequalled example of candour, gentleness, universal tenderness and love. The author of our faith set an example of benevolent activity. We should strive to imitate these examples and so vindicate the honour of our faith, while we 'silence the ignorant talk of foolish men' (1 Pet. 2:15). In this way you will obey the injunction to make the teaching about God our Saviour attractive and to 'let your light shine before men, that they may see your good deeds and praise your Father in heaven' (Matt. 5:16). Beat the world on its own ground. Let your love be more affectionate, your mildness less easily ruffled, show more diligence in your work and in your activity, be more alert and persevering. If a sweet temper and active mind are your talents then they have special value and usefulness for which you will have one day to give account. Carefully guard against anything that might impair them. Cherish them assiduously, keep them in constant use and directed to their most worthy ends. The latter of these qualities makes it less difficult, and the more pressing therefore on you, to abound at all times in the Lord's work and to produce in plenty the kind of good fruit which people will be most ready to admit is excellent, understanding as they do its nature.

If, on the other hand, you are aware that you are naturally a rough and hard individual soured by disappointments, or stimulated by prosperity, or quick in expression and impatient of contradiction, or if, for whatever reason, you have become peevish or waspish in manner, or harsh and severe in speech, remember that these defects are not incompatible with an ability to perform acts of great kindness. Even if your character has been so influenced by bad habits that your soul seems completely coloured by these inclinations to do wrong, do not despair. Remember that God has promised to 'remove from you your heart of stone and give you a heart of flesh' (Ezek. 36:26) whose natural property is to be tender and sensitive. Pray in an earnest and persevering manner for grace to behave in this way. Beware of taking bad moods for granted under the idea that they are the sort of imperfections seen in the best of men. They are only minor occurrences, occasional, hasty and transient outbursts, when you are taken off your guard. This is not so. Do not excuse or permit them in yourself as being simply warm fervour for religion and goodness which you admit is now and then liable to carry you into making an over-severe judgment or sharp reproof.

Examine yourself very strictly and since there is much room for self-deception it may help to consult a close friend and unburden yourself honestly to him; ask for his opinion of your behaviour and state. Our unwillingness to do this often reveals to others that secretly we distrust our own character and conduct. Instead of finding excuses for our evil moods, we should try to make ourselves the more aware of how wrong they are. It helps to be reminded regularly that these unruly and boorish moods are in direct contrast to the meekness and gentleness of the Lord Jesus and that Christians are firmly and repeatedly instructed to model their lives on Him in these particulars. Consider just how much these bitter moods must break in upon and destroy the peace and comfort of those around you. Remember also that your Christian witness is at stake. Take great care not to discredit and thus disgust those whom you ought to conciliate. By conveying an unfavourable impression of your principles and character you may be guilty of putting a stumbling-block in the path of another, and thereby hindering 'the gospel of Christ' (1 Cor. 9:12), the advancement of which should be your constant concern.

Having come to the full understanding of your disease, and how malignant it is, watch and fight against it. Beware lest it breaks out in action. Go out of your way to be courteous and kind and you will gradually discover that the performance of these acts brings a pleasure hitherto unknown. But remember that the Christian is not to be satisfied with the world's veneer of good behaviour, but that his 'Love must be sincere' (Rom. 12:9). Examine yourself in order to find out whether your unChristian moods, which you would like to eradicate, are not being maintained by your selfishness and pride. Strive to subdue them. Get used to seeing our careless and inconsiderate world as being in imminent peril, even though it is ignorant of its danger. Ponder this moving scene until it has roused your pity. Such pity, while it softens the heart with Christian love, also gives rise to an attitude of sympathy and kindness.

Among men of the world, a kindly youth will often, as we

noted previously, become insensitive and sullen. But it is the work of a Christian father in a person's life to reverse this order. It is a pleasure to witness this renovation so that as life advances, sharpness of temper is gradually smoothed and roughnesses are mellowed. The one in which these changes occur experiences an increasing measure of the comfort which he diffuses aware of the heavenly influences within him, looks up with gratitude to the one who has placed this principle of love in his heart.

Do not let it be thought that I have been disparaging of friendly and useful qualities when these have not been prompted and governed by a religious principle. I concede that those who are living in the exercise of these qualities are worthy of commendation. In the words of Scripture, 'they have received their reward' (Matt. 6:16). They have it in an inner satisfaction, which is usually inspired by a sweet temper and also home and social comforts. They are always beloved in private, and respected in public life. But devoid of religion, if the word of God is to be believed, 'no-one can enter the kingdom of God' (John 3:5). Never let it be forgotten that true practical Christianity consists in devoting the heart and life to God, in being governed by a desire to know and fulfil His will and in endeavouring to live to His glory. Where these essential prerequisites are missing, however likeable the individual may be, however creditable and respectable among men, he cannot be labelled as Christian.

But this, however, is a matter between God and a man's own conscience and we must always remember the injunction to be generous in judging the motives of others, while we are strict and severe in questioning our own. We are only too prone to go along with the good opinion which, however untrue, others hold about us, and though we may recognise secretly that their esteem is unfounded and their praises undeserved, we gradually allow ourselves to accept their judgment of us and, finally, feel injured when these false commendations are contradicted or withheld.

There is, however, another danger against which it is necessary to warn Christians. In trying to fulfil this obligation, let them watch out. Having set out with right principles, they lose them insensibly as they progress. Having set out with a sincere and earnest desire to promote the glory of God, their minds may become so taken up with the pursuit of their object that the true motive of their action is either lost altogether or loses much of its life and vigour.

The path of a Christian is beset with dangers. On the one hand, he rightly fears an inactive and unprofitable life, while on the other, with good reason, he dreads the loss of his spirituality. Does the Christian find within himself a steady and growing coldness and unease concerning religious things? And has he grounds to understand that this coldness and unease are due to his being over-occupied in worldly business or to his being too keen on worldly pursuits? Let him carefully and prayerfully examine the state of his own heart, and seriously and impartially survey his priorities. If he finds himself earnestly and seriously pursuing wealth, dignity or reputation, and these things engage many of his thoughts, and if also success in this area gladdens, while disappointments dispirit and distress his mind, then he has good grounds to condemn himself. 'No-one can serve two masters' (Matt. 6:24). The world is clearly in control of his heart and it is no wonder that he finds himself dead to spiritual things.

In those situations where the pursuit of a particular line in business could result in a considerable increase in riches, position or honour, let him soberly and fairly examine whether the pursuit can be justified. Asking the advice of a wise friend would be a great help. Failure to do this might lead him to distrust the reasonableness of the proposed schemes. In such a case as this, we have good cause to distrust ourselves. We may comfort ourselves with the thought that we are prompted by a desire to promote the glory of God and the happiness of our fellows. It is likely that beneath this plausible mask we hide from ourselves perhaps better than from others, an excessive attachment to the splendour and transient distinctions of this life. As this attachment gains a foothold, we shall find that our perceptions and feelings for heavenly things will subside proportionately. Even in less questionable circumstances where there is good reason to believe that there is still a flaw, let us examine carefully the whole of our conduct in order to discover whether we are living a life in breach or omission of some known duty.

In consequence, could it have pleased God to withdraw from us the influence of His Holy Spirit? Look closely as to whether the duties of self-examination, secret and public prayer, the reading of Scripture and the other means of grace have not been omitted or only performed perfunctorily. If this is indeed the case, do not make excuses for such interruptions and curtailments. It is very likely that even our worldly affairs will not go any better because of this encroachment on the time which should be dedicated to God's more immediate service and to the cultivation of our spiritual lives. Evidence of the effects of this fatal negligence will soon be evident in our hearts and behaviour.

Let us, as we make this self-examination, determine whether objects which engross us are really appropriate for us. If they are, let us consider whether they perhaps consume a larger share of our time than is really required and whether, without being negligent, we might not satisfy their claims, and yet have an increased amount of freedom to devote to religion's observance.

If we honestly conclude that we cannot give these worldly objectives less of our time then let us at least endeavour to give them less of our hearts so that the set of our desires and feelings may be more spiritual and that at all times we may be more aware of God's presence, and alert to unseen realities. We shall then accord with Scripture's description of true Christians who 'live by faith, not by sight' (2 Cor. 5:7), and have their 'citizenship in heaven' (Phil. 3:20).

At all times guard against the temptation to lower our standards to the level of our condition, instead of endeavouring to bring ourselves up to the level of our standards. Recognise at all times the worst in ourselves and be suitably affected by it, not making excuses for ourselves, but having always a deep conviction of our slowness and lack of skill in religious matters and a proper awareness of our frailty and many weaknesses. This is a right attitude for us who are commanded to 'work out your salvation with fear and trembling' (Phil. 2:12). It stimulates constant and earnest prayer. It produces that soberness, humility, tenderness, meek manner and circumspection which are so eminently characteristic of a true Christian.

There is much in Scripture to console the believer at this stage. '. . . those who hope in the Lord will renew their strength' (Isa. 40:31). 'Blessed are those who mourn, for they will be comforted' (Matt. 5:4). Such divine assurances soothe and encourage the Christian's disturbed and dejected mind, diffusing a sense of holy composure. The commotion within his soul subsides and he is filled with peace, hope and love. If a feeling of undeserved kindness brings tears to his eyes, they are tears of reconciliation and joy. At the same time, a warm sense of gratitude moves him outward to his daily work, resolved with God's help to live henceforth a more diligent and exemplary life to the glory of God, and longing meanwhile for that blessed time, when being 'liberated from its bondage to decay' (Rom. 8:21) he will be able to render to God a purer and more acceptable service.

Section V
Some other grand defects in the practical system of the bulk of nominal Christians

We have looked somewhat inadequately at the religion of most nominal Christians and their fundamental errors regarding the nature of Christianity with its many harmful effects. In closing this survey there are just a few others to which we should draw attention.

In the first place, it is obvious by their principles and from their behaviour that most nominal Christians have an entirely inadequate idea of sin. We find everywhere that religion is allowed to become no more than a form of policeman. So the guilt of actions is estimated not by the proportion in which, according to Scripture, they offend God, but by that in which they are injurious to society. Murder, theft, fraud in all its shapes, and some forms of lying are manifestly injurious to social happiness. How different, therefore, in the moral scale is the place they hold compared with idolatry, general irreligion, swearing, drinking, fornication, lasciviousness, sensuality, excessive dissipation and, in certain circumstances, to pride, wrath, malice and revenge!

The way that we speak of these failings proves our willingness to look upon them as matters of small account, and sins which are not injurious to the community. We invent for them diminutive and qualifying terms, which, if not a sign of approval and goodwill, are at least proof of our tendency to regard them indulgently. Free thinkers, gallantry, jollity and a thousand similar phrases might be produced as examples. But it should be noted that no such gentle qualifying terms are used in connection with minor theft, fraud, forgery, or any offences committed by men against their fellows and in whose suppression we are personally interested.

There is no denying the charge. In the case of any question of honour or honesty, we are penetrating in our discernment and relentless in judgment. No allowance is made for the temptation's suddenness or strength. One single failure is presumed to imply absence of any moral or honourable principle. The memory is very retentive for such and the man's character is ruined for life. The merest suspicion of having once offended can scarcely be overlooked. But in the case of sins against God, such attitudes do not apply. A man may go on, regularly committing known sins, yet the inference is not drawn that he can have no religious principle. On the contrary, we say of him, 'his behaviour is not quite as it should be, but his heart is in the right place.'

But in God's word, actions are estimated by a far less accommodating standard. We do not read of little sins. Much of the Sermon on the Mount, which many of these

107

whom we are condemning admire, is directed expressly against such a dangerous misconception. There is no distinction made between the rich and the poor. There is not one scale of morals for the higher and another for the lower classes of society. Indeed, the former are distinctly warned that their condition in life is the more dangerous because of the greater number of temptations to which they are exposed. Idolatry, fornication, lasciviousness, drunkenness, revellings, inordinate affection, are all classed by the apostle with theft, murder and whatever we hold in even greater abomination. Concerning them all, Scripture pronounces that 'those who live like this will not inherit the kingdom of God' (Gal. 5:19–21; Col. 3:5–9).

The example which we have given of the lax system of these nominal Christians betrays a fatal absence of that which is the very foundation of all religion. Their scant ideas of the guilt and evil of sin reveals an utter lack of a proper reverence for Almighty God. This basic principle is rightly termed in Scripture, 'the beginning of wisdom'; there is no other single quality which the sacred writers studiously attempt to impress upon the human heart (Job 28:28; Ps. 111:10; Prov. 1:7, 9:10).

Scripture sees sin as rebellion against God's sovereignty and every different act of it equally violates His law, and if persevered in disclaims His supremacy. To the inconsiderate and light-hearted this doctrine may seem harsh, as they bask in the sunshine of worldly prosperity and lull themselves into false security. 'But the day of the Lord will come like a thief. The heavens will disappear with a roar; the elements will be destroyed by fire, and the earth and everything in it will be laid bare. Since everything will be destroyed in this way, what kind of people ought you to be? You ought to live holy and godly lives' (2 Pet. 3:10–11). 'The wicked return to the grave, all the nations that forget God' (Ps. 9:17).

It should also be noted that these awful denunciations against sin derive additional weight from the fact that they represent not merely a judicial sentence which God might remit through His mercy, but as arising in the course of

108

nature, and as happening in the way of natural consequence as cause and effect. It is stated that the kingdom of God and the kingdom of Satan are both set up in the world, and that we must belong to one or the other. 'We know that we have passed from death to life' (1 John 3:14). 'For he has rescued us from the dominion of darkness and brought us into the kingdom of the Son he loves' (Col. 1:13). We have become 'the children' and 'the subjects of God'. While on earth, we love His day, His service, His people, we 'speak good of his name;' and abound in His service. Even in this life we share something of His image which will one day be perfected. We will wake in His 'likeness' and receive 'an inheritance that can never perish, spoil or fade – kept in heaven for you' (1 Pet. 1:4).

Sinners, on the other hand, are said to 'belong to your father, the devil' (John 8:44). While on earth, they are his children, and servants who are called to do his works, and are the subjects of his kingdom. Eventually Jesus the Saviour will become their judge, and pronounce the dreaded sentence, 'Depart from me, you who are cursed, into the eternal fire prepared for the devil and his angels' (Matt. 25:41).

Could these declarations fail to strike terror or at least excite serious fears and apprehension in the most light-hearted individual? But men's imaginations are so prone to seek false hopes in the very face of such a positive declaration. We cannot believe that God would in fact be so severe. This was how Satan deluded our first parents. 'You will not surely die' (Gen. 3:4).

Had these rash men lived in the antediluvian world, would they have thought it possible that God would carry out His threat and send a flood? Yet the flood came and this awful example of God's anger against sin was recorded in Scripture for our instruction.

The world at that time was perhaps not very different from what is to be found in many of the European nations. It was a selfish, luxurious, irreligious and inconsiderate world. They were called, but they would not listen; they were warned, but they would not believe. In the words of the Gospel writer, 'people were eating and drinking, marrying and giving in marriage . . . and they knew nothing about what would happen until the flood came and took them all away' (Matt. 24:38–9).

Once again what we have been describing reveals a most inadequate conception of what it means to become a true Christian and what is involved in preparing us for the delights of heaven. The general idea seems to be that a person born in a country of which Christianity is the established religion is a Christian. We do not therefore look for any positive evidence to that effect, but simply take it for granted until evidence is produced to the contrary. And we are very slow to listen to what our conscience would tell us and clever at justifying what is clearly wrong. We make excuses where we cannot justify and enlarge upon the merits of what is moderately commendable. We flatter ourselves that our bad habits are only occasional acts and blow up one good deed into a life of virtue. We do not suspect our true condition so we do not set about doing some serious self-examination. We only receive in a confused and hurried way occasional indications of our danger: such as when sickness, the loss of a friend, or the commission of some rather more noteworthy misdeed awaken our consciences rather more than is usual.

So most people completely overlook the fact that a Christian has a great work to execute in conforming himself to the pattern of his Lord and Master, through the work of the Holy Spirit. They are unaware of the obstacles in their way and of the enemies which impede their progress, and they forget the ample provision that has been made to enable them to surmount the one and to conquer the other. The pictures in Scripture of the Christian's state on earth indicate 'a race' and 'a warfare', that it is necessary to rid himself of anything that impedes his progress in the race and to avail himself of God's armour for victory in the warfare, are, to these nominal Christians, figures devoid of meaning.

But all this is only nominal Christianity and in the language of Scripture, Christianity is not a geographical but

110

a moral term. It is not a matter of being a native of a Christian country, but the possessor of a peculiar nature, with the qualities and properties which belong to it.

Furthermore, it is a state into which we are not born, but into which we must be translated. It is not a nature which we inherit, but one into which we are to be created anew. It is to the undeserved grace of God that we must be indebted for attaining this new and spiritual nature and to acquire and make good this great work in us we are commanded to 'work out your salvation with fear and trembling' (Phil. 2:12). We are constantly reminded that this involves hard, difficult work, vigilance, unceasing effort and great patience. Even towards the close of a long life of active service, or cheerful suffering, we find Paul declaring that he considered bodily self-denial and mental discipline to be essential for his very safety. Christians worthy of the name, are represented as qualified 'to share in the inheritance of the saints in the kingdom of light' (Col. 1:12); as waiting 'for our Lord Jesus Christ to be revealed' (1 Cor. 1:7); and as looking for 'the day of God and speed its coming' (2 Pet. 3:12).

Being aware of the absolute importance and arduous nature of the service in which he is engaged, the true Christian sets about his task with vigour and diligence. It is as though he has fled from a country in which the plague is raging. He does not consider it sufficient simply to cross the boundary, but he would rather remove any doubt and put himself well away from the infection. He is prepared to meet difficulties and is not discouraged when they occur. Having been warned of his many adversaries, he is not alarmed or lacking in defence when they approach. He knows that the beginnings of every new road may be expected to be rough and painful, but is assured that they will soon seem smoother, and become indeed 'pleasant ways and . . . paths of peace' (Prov. 3:17).

For such a state the description of pilgrim and stranger is very appropriate and all the other descriptions and illustrations by which Christians are represented in Scripture have these same connotations. Indeed, there is no other way in which a Christian's state on earth is more frequently featured in God's word than by that of a journey. The Christian is travelling on business through a strange country in which he has been ordered to carry out his work diligently and to make speed homeward. The fruits which he notices beside the road he picks cautiously and he drinks moderately from the streams. He is thankful when the sun shines, and the road is pleasant, but if it is rough and wet he is not unduly concerned, for he is only a traveller. He is prepared for vicissitudes and knows that he must expect to meet with them in this world's stormy and uncertain climate. But he is going to a 'better country' with cloudless skies and undisturbed serenity. He notices from experience, that the fewer the creature comforts, the less he is disposed to loiter and if for a while the way is less attractive, he can comfort himself with the thought that he is that much farther along the road.

When the going is easier he observes his surroundings, admires the beauty, investigates the unusual and thankfully accepts and enjoys the refreshments offered to him. He is not stand-offish or aloof from the local inhabitants. He does not permit pleasure, curiosity, or socialising to absorb his time, but remains intent on completing the business he has in hand, and on continuing the journey that he has been set. He knows that to the very end of life, his journey will be through a country in which he has many enemies, that his path is endangered by traps, that temptations crowd in on him to seduce him from his course, or check his progress in it. The very air induces drowsiness so that to the very end he will have to be circumspect and alert.

Frequently he examines his whereabouts to see how he has progressed and whether or not he is travelling in the right direction. Sometimes he makes considerable progress, at others he advances but slowly and too often he fears with reason that he has gone backwards. Now cheered with hope and gladdened by success, at other times he is disquieted by doubts and damped by disappointments. To nominal Christians religion is a dull uniform thing, and they have no idea of the desires, disappointments, hopes, fears, joys and sorrows which it calls forth in the individual believer. In the true Christian all is life and motion, and his great work calls forth the various passions of the soul.

Our review of the character of most nominal Christians has yielded abundant evidence that they lack that great constituent of the true Christian character, the love of God. Concerning the signs and evidence of true feeling there can be little doubt, but if you examine the character and language of these persons you will be compelled to acknowledge that so far as love of God is concerned, there is no evidence to be found of the very fact that these nominal Christians take no pleasure in the service and worship of God, which in itself is highly significant. The acts of devotion resemble less the free-will offerings of a grateful heart than the forced and reluctant homage, exacted by some hard master from his oppressed dependents, and paid with a cold sullenness and slavish apprehension. God brought this same charge against His ungrateful people of old who called Him sovereign and Father, and yet withheld from Him the regard which such names would indicate as His due. In like manner we are satisfied to offer to Almighty God our Saviour a dull sham, empty gratitude which we should be ashamed to offer to one of our fellows.

It can be of very great value to us if we can make a habit of keeping the first and great commandment in the front of our minds. 'Love the Lord your God with all your heart and with all your soul and with all your mind' (Matt. 22:37). This motive, effective and vigorous in nature would, like a master spring, put and maintain in action all the complicated movements of the human soul. It would rapidly scotch many questions concerning certain activities which are only really a problem to those who submit only reluctantly to God's command. Fear deters from obvious crimes, and self-interest will bribe some to perform acts of service, but it is the peculiar glory and characteristic of love to show itself in ten thousand little and undefinable acts of painstaking attentiveness, which love alone can pay. Love goes beyond reason's deductions. It does not take refuge in casuistry, it does not demand proof that one action would

113

injure and offend, or another benefit or please the object of affection. The slightest hint or suggestion suffices to make it veer away from the former and fly eagerly to the latter.

While we have seen the degree to which most nominal Christians are lacking in love for God, the strength of their love towards their fellows is often seen to be praiseworthy. The many benevolent institutions to be found in this country may be used as our argument in favour of this opinion. Much of what might have been argued in the discussion of this topic has already been raised in communication with the subject of friendly temperaments and useful lives, unconnected with any religious principle. What was stated then may serve to lower, in the present instance, the lofty pretensions of these nominal Christians and we shall mention later another consideration, whose effect must be to reduce still further their claims. Meanwhile, suffice it to remark that active philanthropy must not be assumed simply on the grounds of generosity to the poor, by one who is in no way incommoded by his liberality. No luxury is forgone and no inconvenience experienced.

Perhaps we should reach a less favourable but no less fair conclusion if we were to try these individuals by those tests which the apostle stated are the less ambiguous indications of true philanthropy. The strength of every passion is to be judged by its ability to overcome an opposite passion. How does present-day benevolence stand the shock, when it comes up against our pride, vanity, self-love, self-interest, love of ease or of pleasure, our ambition, or our craving for worldly praise? Does it make us self-denying so that we can be generous in relieving others? Does it make us persevere in doing good in spite of ingratitude? Have we only pity for the ignorance, prejudice, or malice which misrepresent our conduct, or misconstrue our motives? Does it cause us to refrain from doing what we consider could result in harm to one of our fellows, even though that harm results, not from our behaviour, but from his own obstinacy or weakness? Are we slow to believe things said about our neighbour which are harmful to him? If we are forced to believe it, are we disposed to keep quiet and as far as is right, seek to

114

make amends rather than guard the news or aggravate it?

Suppose we have an opportunity to perform an act of kindness, to one who because of pride or vanity would be loth to receive, or at least be known to receive, a favour from us. Should we attempt, in honesty, to reduce his mind and that of others from the idea that what we were doing was meritorious and in the way of enabling him to be less reluctant to receive what was proffered? Can we, from motives of kindness, lay ourselves open to the charge of being lacking in spirit, penetration, or foresight? Do we tell another his faults, when in doing so, even though he benefit by it, embarrassment or pain is occasioned to ourselves, and his regard for us or his opinion is thereby diminished of our judgment? Are we able to suppress a rejoinder which would wound another, when its utterance would gratify our vanity, and its suppression may harm our reputation as a wit? If we have advised a particular line of conduct to someone or have pointed out the likely harm resulting from the opposite course, and if our advice has not been heeded, are we genuinely saddened when our predictions of evil come about? Does our love surpass our envy, jealousy and rivalry? Are we quick to notice and grasp an honest opportunity to promote another's interests? In the case of our enemies, does our attitude accord with Scripture in that we love? Are we meek when provoked, ready to forgive, and quick to forget injuries? Can we, in all sincerity, 'bless those who curse you, pray for those who ill-treat you' (Luke 6:28)? When God searches our hearts does He find a real spirit of forgiveness, as evidenced not only by our forbearing to avenge an injury but even from telling anyone how badly we have been done by? And lastly, are we not only content to return good for evil to our enemies, but when they succeed or fail independently of any contribution from us, can we be not only content, but feel pleasure in their prosperity, or sorrow for their distress?

These are only a few examples of the characteristic features seen in a life ruled by benevolence. Yet even these may serve to show us just how most nominal Christians fall short of what Scripture requires. The truth is, we too infrequently remember the right level of Scripture morality, and in consequence are therefore liable to value ourselves by the standards which we attained. A little more self-knowledge would have convinced us that we were falling far short of the prescribed standard. On the very difficult question to which we have just referred, regarding the forgiveness and love of enemies, our Saviour points out that we should follow His example. He states that being kind and courteous to those who are entitled to such is not evidence of Christian benevolence on our part. He goes further and adds, 'Be perfect, therefore, as your heavenly Father is perfect' (Matt. 5:48).

Section VI
Grand defect – Neglect of the peculiar doctrines of Christianity

The major deficiency in the practice of these nominal Christians is their neglect of all the doctrines peculiar to the religion which they profess – the corruption of human nature, atonement by our Saviour, and the sanctifying work of the Holy Spirit. This is the great difference between nominal Christians and true Christians.

There are many who have led a life of dissipation and indulged all their natural appetites, then are for some reason made aware of the infinite importance of religion.

Sickness, perhaps, or the loss of a friend or loved one, or some adverse fortune, depresses them and makes them aware of the precariousness of human life. They start to look for some more stable foundation of happiness than is offered by this world. After only a little self-examination they become aware that they must have offended God. So they resolve to set about the work of reformation. Here the fatal effects of the prevailing ignorance of the real nature of Christianity and the neglect of its unique doctrines become apparent. These people want to reform, but they are unaware of the real nature of their disease or its proper

116

treatment. Indeed, they are aware that they must 'cease to do evil, and learn to do well'; that they must give up their sinful habits and attend to religious duties. But being unaware of the severity of their disease, of the perfect cure provided by the Gospel, or of the way in which that cure is brought about:

> They do but skim and film the ulcerous place,
> While rank corruption, mining all within,
> Infects unseen.

It happens only too easily with these people that where they do not at an early stage give up their attempt at reformation and relapse into their old sinful habits, they make a partial amendment and persuade themselves that it is a thorough change. They now consider that they have a right to the benefits of Christianity. Unable to bring their practice up to the right standard they lower their standard to the level of their practice. They are content with their present attainment, deluded by self-satisfaction and the favourable comments of their friends.

Others, perhaps, go farther than this. Dread of the wrath to come has sunk deeper into their hearts and for a time they strive with all their might against their evil propensities and to walk the path of duty without stumbling. Again and again they resolve, yet again and again they break their resolutions. Every endeavour is foiled, and they become increasingly convinced of their own moral weakness and of the corrupting power within. They are tempted in consequence to give up in despair and accept their wretched captivity, believing it impossible to break their chains. While this conflict rages, their daily life is sad and comfortless, they are depressed and tearful. These people are pursuing the right object, but they have missed the way to get there. The path they are now treading is not the one the Gospel provides to conduct them to true holiness.

Under these circumstances people will often turn to religious instruction. They look at the works of our modern theologians and, as well as they can, examine the advice addressed to men in their situation. It goes something like this: 'Be very sorry for your sins, and cease from their practice, but do not be so concerned. Christ died for the sins of the whole world. Try hard, fulfil your duties faithfully and do not neglect your religious observances; have no fear for in the end all will be well, and you will at last obtain God's forgiveness through the merits of Jesus Christ. And where your own strength is insufficient you will be aided by His Holy Spirit. Meanwhile, you cannot do better than read carefully those books of practical divinity that will instruct you in Christian living. There are plenty of these available and diligent study of them will gradually make you proficient in the Gospel's lessons.'

But Scriptures (and with them the Church of England) call upon those who are in such circumstances to renew the whole foundation of their religion. In accord with Scripture, that Church calls upon them first of all to give thanks and praise to the one who, though they are undeserving, has awakened them from the sleep of death; then to fall down before the cross of Christ in humble repentance and deep self-loathing, resolving solemnly to forsake all their sins and rely on God's grace alone for power to keep their resolution. In this way alone are they assured that all their sins will be blotted out and that they will receive from above a holy and spiritual life. The basis and authority for this advice are found in God's word. 'Believe in the Lord Jesus, and you will be saved' (Acts 16:31). 'No-one', says our Saviour, 'comes to the Father except through me' (John 14:6). 'I am the true vine . . . No branch can bear fruit by itself; it must remain in the vine. Neither can you bear fruit unless you remain in me. If a man remains in me and I in him, he will bear much fruit; apart from me, you can do nothing' (John 15:1–5). 'For it is by grace you have been saved, through faith – and this not from yourselves, it is the gift of God – not by works, so that no-one can boast. For we are God's workmanship, created in Christ Jesus to do good works' (Eph. 2:8–10).

This point cannot be overstressed. On this the whole of Christianity turns. There have been some who have thought that the wrath of God was something to deprecate and that His favour could be conciliated by austerities, penances, forms and ceremonies and external observances. If men acknowledge God's moral government, then they must also acknowledge that vice must offend and virtue delight Him. In short they must assent to Scripture when it declares, 'without holiness no-one will see the Lord' (Heb. 12:14). But the major distinction between a true Christian and a nominal one concerns the nature of his holiness, and the way in which it is to be obtained. The views held by the latter, of the nature of holiness, are to a degree all inadequate and they believe that it is obtained by their own natural unassisted efforts. If they admit in a vague sort of way that it involves the assistance of the Holy Spirit, it is quite clear on talking to them, that in practical terms this is not what they depend on. But the holiness to which the true Christian directs his desires is no other than the restoration of the image of God in his life. Far from attaining it by his own strength, all his hopes of possessing it rest completely on God's assurances of the working of the Holy Spirit in those who believe the Good News of Jesus Christ. He knows therefore that this holiness is not to precede his reconciliation to God, and so be its cause, but to follow it, and be its effect. That, in short, it is by faith in Christ alone that he is to be justified in the sight of God, delivered from the condition of a child of wrath and a slave of Satan. He is adopted into God's family and becomes an heir of God and a joint heir with Christ, entitled to all the privileges which belong to this high relationship. These involve in this life, by the spirit of grace, a partial renewal after the image of his Creator and, hereafter, the more perfect possession of the divine likeness and an eternal and glorious inheritance.

And so, in obedience to the Gospel, the true Christian first comes to possess the new life which leads to growth in holiness. In order to grow in grace, he must continue to study, finding as he contemplates the special doctrines contained in the Gospel and also in the life, character and sufferings of our Saviour, the basis for all practical wisdom, with an inexhaustible store of instructions and motives. It is the neglect of these special doctrines that lies at the root of most of the errors of professed Christians. With mighty truths in view, the littleness of their dwarfish morality would be put to shame. In no way would they be made to harmonise with their inadequate conceptions of the wretchedness and danger of their natural state. A state represented in Scripture as having moved God's compassion so powerfully that He sent His only begotten Son to rescue us. Where now their low conceptions of the value of the soul, when means like these were taken to redeem it? Where their inadequate conceptions of the guilt of sin, for which in God's wisdom it required an atonement no less costly than that of the blood of the only begotten Son of God? How can they reconcile their low standard of Christian practice with the representation of our being 'a temple of the Holy Spirit' (1 Cor. 6:19) and 'rescued . . . from the dominion of darkness and brought . . . into the kingdom of the Son he loves' (Col. 1:13).

The doctrines peculiar to the Gospel having been admitted, then some obvious conclusions follow. To neglect these important truths is unpardonable, because they are clearly and repeatedly applied in Scripture to the subject in question, and the whole superstructure of Christian morality is based on them. Sometimes these truths are represented in Scripture, generally, as furnishing Christians with a vigorous and ever-present principle of universal obedience. And our learning of the lesson of heavenly wisdom is still further stimulated by almost every particular Christian duty being occasionally traced as to its proper source. They are everywhere represented as warming the hearts of the people of God on earth with continual admiration, thankfulness, love and joy; as triumphing over the attack of the last great enemy, and as calling forth afresh in heaven the ardent effusions of their unexhausted gratitude.

If we would indeed be filled with 'all spiritual wisdom and understanding' (Col. 1:9), if we would 'live a life worthy of the Lord and . . . please him in every way: bearing fruit in every good work, growing in the knowledge of God' (Col. 1:10). This is where we should be looking! '. . . let us throw off everything that hinders and the sin that so easily entangles, and let us run with perseverance the race marked out for us. Let us fix our eyes on Jesus, the author and perfecter of our faith, who for the joy set before him endured the cross, scorning its shame, and sat down at the right hand of the throne of God' (Heb. 12:1–2).

This is the best way to learn the importance of Christianity. How little does it deserve to be treated in such a trivial and superficial way, as indeed it is in these days by most nominal Christians. They think it will suffice, and be equally pleasing to God, to be religious in any way, and by any system. What folly to risk the soul on such a venture, in direct contradiction to reason's dictates and the express declaration of the word of God! '. . . how shall we escape if we ignore such a great salvation?' (Heb. 2:3).

Fix our eyes on Jesus!

This is the best place to learn that an absolute and unconditional surrender of soul and body to the will and service of God is not only our duty but also is sensible. 'You are not your own; you were bought at a price,' and must therefore make it your chief concern to 'honour God with your body' (1 Cor. 6:19–20). Could we be so base as to make any reserves in our returns of service to such a gracious Saviour? If we have previously talked of condoning some actions which are wrong, can we now bear to mention such a thing, or serve to ourselves the right to practise 'little' sins? The very suggestion of such an idea fills us with indignation and shame.

Fix our eyes on Jesus!

Here also we get a clear idea of the guilt of sin, and how hateful it must be to a God of perfect holiness. 'Your eyes are too pure to look on evil' (Hab. 1:13). When we see that, rather than let sin go unpunished, 'He . . . did not spare his own Son, but gave him up for us all ' (Rom. 8:32). 'Yet it was the Lord's will to crush him and cause him to suffer'

(Isa. 53:10), for our sakes. Impenitent sinners have a vain hope of escaping heaven's vengeance as they buoy themselves up with desperate dreams of a benign deity!

Rather than that we should undergo the suffering of hell, God's Son Himself, who 'did not consider equality with God something to be grasped' (Phil. 2:6) consented to take upon Himself our degraded nature, with all its physical weaknesses. He became 'a man of sorrows' (Isa. 53:3) who did not hide His face 'from mocking and spitting' (Isa. 50:6) and was 'pierced for our transgressions, he was crushed for our iniquities' (Isa. 53:5). In the end He endured death's sharpness 'even death on a cross!' (Phil. 2:8) in order to rescue 'us from the coming wrath' (1 Thess. 1:10) and open the kingdom of heaven to all believers.

Fix our eyes on Jesus!

This is where we learn to grow in the love of God! The certainty of His pity and love towards repenting sinners, undisputedly demonstrated, chases away all fear and lays the foundation in us for a reciprocal feeling. And while we contemplate steadily this wonderful transaction and with all its different aspects, the amazing truth, that God 'did not spare his own Son, but gave him up for us all' (Rom. 8:32), if we are not completely insensitive then feelings of admiration, preference, hope, trust and joy must spring up within us. These will be tempered by reverential fear, and softened and quickened by overflowing gratitude. An abiding desire will fill us to try to please our mighty Saviour. Whenever we are conscious that we have offended our gracious Lord, one thought of the great work of redemption will suffice to stir our consciences. We shall feel deep concern, grief mingled with shame, for having behaved so unworthily towards one who has been infinite in kindness to us. We shall not rest till we have reason to hope that He is reconciled to us again. We shall watch our hearts and future conduct with increased care lest we should offend Him again. The feelings and dispositions which have been enumerated are the infallible indicators and the constituents of love.

The assiduous and frequent consideration of the great Gospel doctrines must tend to produce and nurture in our minds the principle of the love of Christ.

Much has been already said concerning the love of our fellows and it has been clearly stated to be the Christian's indispensable and characteristic duty. It remains only to remark that this grace can be cultivated nowhere with greater benefit than at the foot of the cross. Nowhere can we reflect with more effect our Saviour's dying injunction to exercise this virtue: 'A new command I give you: Love one another. As I have loved you' (John 13:34). Nowhere can the apostle's admonition affect us more powerfully: 'Be kind and compassionate to one another, forgiving each other, just as in Christ God forgave you' (Eph. 4:32). Just the picture of man as involved in one common ruin and the offer of deliverance held out to all by God's Son giving of Himself to pay the price of our reconciliation, produces a sympathy towards our fellow-creatures. Pity for an un-thinking world adds to this feeling so that our enmities soften and melt away. We are ashamed of dwelling over petty injuries which we may have suffered, when we con-sider what the Son of God who 'committed no sin, and no deceit was found in his mouth' (1 Pet. 2:22) patiently underwent. Our hearts become tender while we contem-plate this signal act of loving kindness and we long to imitate what we can only admire. A lively principle of increased and active charity takes hold of us and we set off speedily, desiring to tread in our Master's steps and to show our gratitude for His unmerited goodness, by bearing each other's burdens, and abounding in good works.

Fix our eyes on Jesus!

He was meek and lowly, and the study of His character is the best way to learn the lessons of humility. As we contemplate the work of redemption, we become more and more aware of our state of natural darkness, helplessness

123

and misery, from which at such a price, it was necessary to ransom us. We become increasingly conscious that we are utterly unworthy of all the amazing condescension and love which have been shown us. The callousness of our tenderest feelings shames us as do the poor results of our most active services. Such considerations abate our pride, reduce our opinion of ourselves, and naturally temper our demands upon others. We are less disposed to insist on respect for our persons and authority, which we naturally covet. We are less sensitive to slight and resent it less hotly. Less irritable and prone to be dissatisfied, we are more gentle and courteous. We are not required literally to behave in the same humiliating way as our Saviour Himself. 'Now that I, your Lord and Teacher, have washed your feet, you also should wash one another's feet' (John 13:14), but the spirit of His remark applies to us 'no servant is greater than his master' (John 13:16). We should bear this truth in mind especially when called upon to discharge some duty, or patiently to bear some ill treatment which will wound our pride and we are likely to fall in the world's estimation. At the same time sacred Scripture assures us that it is to the powerful operation of the Holy Spirit, purchased for us by the death of Christ, that we must be indebted for the success of all our endeavours to improve in virtue. An appreciation of these truths will keep us from any vanity. It is Scripture's characteristic that by its application all tendency to exalt ourselves is excluded, so that if we really grow in grace, we shall also grow in humility.

Fix our eyes on Jesus!

He 'endured the cross, scorning its shame' (Heb. 12:2). While we steadily contemplate this solemn scene, a spirit of soberness comes over us, which best befits the Christian fighting here on earth. We become aware of the shortness and uncertainty of time, and that it is incumbent upon us to be diligent and make provision for eternity. In such a frame of mind, life's pomps and vanities are put behind us like children's playthings. We lose our relish for a life of gaiety and ambition's race. In the case even of those objects which might more justly claim our attention such as our family arrangements, our plans for life or our business schemes, we become though dutiful, more moderate in pursuit and more indifferent about the outcome. Here also we learn to correct the world's false estimate of things, to venerate the truly excellent and noble and to cultivate that true magnanimity so that we can rise above the smiles or frowns of this world with a dignified composure which no earthly happenings can destroy or ruffle.

Instead of enduring the little inconveniences we may meet from time to time, we are almost ashamed of our many comforts and enjoyments, when we think of Him, who though 'the Lord of glory' (1 Cor. 2:8) had 'nowhere to lay his head' (Matt. 8:20). And if evils of more than ordinary magnitude befall us, we are borne up by reflecting that hereby we are more conformed to the example of our Master. But we must always remember one important difference, that Christ's sufferings were voluntarily borne for our benefit and were probably far more exquisitely agonising than any which we are called upon to experience. Besides, it is a great support to us to know that troubles do not happen to us by chance. They are not even merely the punishment of sin, but the dispensations of a kindly Providence.

Fix our eyes on Jesus!

'The author and perfecter of our faith, who for the joy set before him endured the cross, scorning its shame, and sat down at the right hand of the throne of God' (Heb. 12:2). From the scene of our Saviour's weakness and degradation, we follow Him, in our imagination, into the realms of glory, where he is on the right hand of God; angels, and principalities, and powers being made subject to Him. But though in a different place, He still has the same nature, full of sympathy and love and having died to save 'his people from their sins' (Matt. 1:21), 'he always lives to intercede for them' (Heb. 7:25). Cheered by this inspiring view, the Christian's fainting spirits revive. Under the heaviest burdens he feels reinvigorated and when all around is dark and stormy he can look up to heaven, radiant with hope and gratitude. At such a time dangers cannot alarm, opposition move, or provocations irritate. He may note as the language of his sober process what in the philosopher would be idle ranting. Since it is only his mortal body which is subject to the darts of fortune, while his spirit, cheered by divine support, remains secure and unassailable, he can sometimes almost triumph at the stake.

But rarely is the Christian elevated with this 'inexpressible and glorious joy' (1 Pet. 1:8). Sadly, emotions of another kind often fill him with grief and confusion and he is conscious of having acted in a manner unworthy of his high calling. Perhaps he has exposed himself to the just censure of a world ready enough to spy out his weakness. However, let him remember that his chief business on earth is not to meditate, but to act. The seeds of moral corruption are prone to spring up within him so that he must watch over his heart with incessant care. He must faithfully fulfil his particular duties and behave himself by following the example of his Master, whose meat and drink it was to do the work of his heavenly Father. He should diligently cultivate the talents which God has entrusted to him and employ them assiduously in doing justice and showing mercy, while he guards against the assaults of the enemy within.

In short, he is to behave in all the common affairs of life like someone who is accountable and whose actions correspond with descriptions in Scripture of Christians who 'eagerly wait for our Lord Jesus Christ to be revealed' (1 Cor. 1:7). He will often ask himself, 'Am I using my time, my fortune, my bodily and mental powers, so as to be able to give a good account of myself?' Am I making 'the teaching about God our Saviour attractive' (Titus 2:10)? Am I demonstrating that Christ's servants inspired by the love of their Father, which makes their work for Him a service of perfect freedom, are as capable of active and persevering exertion as are the seekers of fame, or the slaves of ambition, or greed?

Without interrupting his work, a Christian may from time to time switch his thoughts to spiritual things and look towards his heavenly advocate, who is always pleading on behalf of His people and supplying them with grace and consolation. If he can gain spiritual refreshment from these glimpses which are 'but a poor reflection' (1 Cor.13:12), what will it be like on the resurrection morning when he awakes to the unclouded vision of celestial glory? So let us not forget that the main distinction between real and nominal Christianity consists chiefly in the different importance assigned to the special teachings found in the Gospel. For nominal Christians, if they admit such teachings they are regarded like the stars in the sky as seen by the naked eye. They occasionally draw forth a transient expression of admiration, when we see their beauty, or hear their distances, magnitudes, or properties described. We may muse sometimes on their possible uses, but however curious as subjects of speculation except in the minds of astrologers, they have no influence on human happiness, or any concern with the course and order of the world. For these nominal Christians it is just so with the Gospel's teachings. For the real Christian, on the other hand, these teachings constitute his true centre of gravity; the very sun of his system! They are the source of light, life, motion and growth! Even the Old Testament itself, though divinely revealed, shines less brightly when seen on its own. But the truths of the Gospel have now been unveiled for us to see and we are invited to look upon and enjoy 'the light of the knowledge of the glory of God in the face of Christ' (2 Cor. 4:6). The words of inspiration best express our highly favoured state: 'And we, who with unveiled faces all reflect the Lord's glory, are being transformed into his likeness with ever-increasing glory, which comes from the Lord, who is the Spirit' (2 Cor. 3:18).

V

ON THE EXCELLENCE OF CHRISTIANITY IN CERTAIN IMPORTANT PARTICULARS. ARGUMENT WHICH RESULTS THENCE IN PROOF OF ITS DIVINE ORIGIN

Having completed an outline of the main features of true Christianity, we can now point out some of its excellent features which confirm its divine origins.

As with all God's works a careful examination makes us better acquainted with their properties, we become more deeply impressed by their excellence. In the last chapter we pointed out the close connection and harmony existing between the doctrines and precepts of Christianity, which is apt to escape the attention of the casual observer. It is self-evident that the corruption of human nature, our reconciliation to God by Christ's atonement and our renewal by the sanctifying influence of the Holy Spirit, are all parts of one whole.

Perhaps, however, it has not been grasped sufficiently that in Christianity's chief practical precepts there is the same essential agreement, the same mutual dependence of one upon another.

The virtues most strongly and repeatedly urged in Scripture, and by which we may gauge our progress in holiness, are our fear and love of God and Christ; our love, kindness and meekness for our fellows, our indifference to the possessions and events of this life, compared with our concern for eternal things and our self-denial and humility. It may be helpful to dwell a little on some of these graces. Take, for example, loving kindness and meekness towards others and notice the solid foundation laid for them in self-denial, moderation as to life's good things, and in humility. Enmity among men arises mainly because of pride and self-importance, the high opinion which men entertain of themselves, and the consequent deference which they demand from others. There is an overvaluation of worldly possessions and of worldly honours and, consequently, a too eager competition of them.

The rough edges of one man rubbing against those of another, tend to injure the works, and disturb the smooth movement of society's machinery. But true Christians find that these roughnesses are being filed down and the wheels smoothly turning in consequence. The religious system of most nominal Christians is satisfied with some appearances of virtue and while it recommends love and good works, it often tolerates pride and vanity. It even tolerates and commends the overvaluation of character and a man's whole being to be absorbed in whatever he is following, be it personal or professional success. But though these latter qualities may in the main be veiled by gentle and gracious manner, they cannot accord with a genuine life of love. Some discontent or ground for jealousy or envy will arise, suspicion will corrode, disappointment sour, some slight or calumny will irritate and provoke reprisals. Some of us learn to disguise our emotions, but these will be our true inner feelings and they will frequently betray themselves when we are off guard, or when we are likely to be discredited for revealing them.

This state in some circles, in which men are scuffling eagerly for the same ends while appearing to be sweetness and complacency, itself has often reminded me of a gaming table. There, every man is intent only on his own table. There, every man is intent only on his own gain. One's good success is another's loss and therefore you can guess what is the general state of mind of the engaged parties. All this, however, does not prevent, in well-bred societies, an exterior of perfect gentleness and good humour. But let the same gaming be carried on among those not so well schooled in the art of disguising their feelings, or in places where people give vent to their real emotions, and every passion will be evident.

But Christianity requires of us such genuine behaviour as will stand God's scrutinising gaze as He 'searches our hearts' (Rom. 8:27). Since the Christian should live in and breathe an atmosphere of charitable thoughts whatever tends to obstruct or foul it is therefore forbidden. It is on these grounds that rivalry is forbidden, because unwittingly it degenerates into envy and because it originates from pride and a desire for self-exaltation. How can we love our neighbour as ourselves, if at the same time we consider him to be our rival and are intent upon surpassing him in whatever is the subject of our competition?

Christianity, again, teaches us not to set our hearts on earthly possessions and honours. In this way it enables us really to love or even forgive those who have been more successful than ourselves in their attainment, or who have by design thwarted our efforts.

Christianity also teaches us not to overvalue human estimation. By so doing we are able to obey the injunction to love sincerely those who, justly or unjustly, may have attacked our reputation and damaged our character. It is not the demonstration, but the reality of meekness and gentleness that is required of Christians.

Another important feature of Christianity is that moral attainments are considered to be of greater consequence than intellectual ones. Virtue excels over knowledge.

The fact that Christianity shows a preference for moral rather than intellectual excellence is not to be praised simply because it is in keeping with her general character, and fits the ends which she has in view. True wisdom is to endeavour to excel in that area where we can really achieve excellence. This consideration alone might be sufficient to direct our efforts to acquiring virtue rather than knowledge. How limited in range is the greatest of human abilities! How scanty are the stores of the richest human knowledge! Those who undeniably have been pre-eminent both naturally and by training instead of thinking that their position is a just basis for praise, have often been the most ready to admit that their outlook was limited and their achievements but moderate. Had they indeed been less candid, this discovery we could not have failed to make for ourselves. Experience furnishes us daily with examples of weakness and error in the wisest and most learned, which should serve to confound the pride of human wisdom.

Not so in morals. Made at first in the likeness of God, we still bear some faint traces of our lofty beginnings, and the Saviour offers us the means of being purified of our corruption, and of once more regaining the image of our heavenly Father (Eph. 2). In love, which is the compendium of almost every virtue, in fortitude, in justice, in humility and in all the other graces of the Christian character we are enabled to attain great heights. If we were but faithful in using the means of grace, the work of the Holy Spirit in our lives, prompting and assisting us, would infallibly bring success to our labours and make us share in God's nature. Let me not be thought to undervalue any of God's gifts or the fruits of human exertion, but do not let these be prized above their proper worth. If one of those little industrious insects, to which we have been well sent for a lesson of diligence and foresight, were to pride itself upon its strength, because it could make off with a larger grain of wheat than any other of its fellow-ants, would we not laugh at such vanity? And is it so very different when weak, short-sighted man prides himself at surpassing others in knowledge and his nature's true dignity and the way to true excellence?

It is not the writer's intention to attempt to vindicate the divine origin of our faith. This task has many times been carried out by far abler advocates. Anxious, however, in my small way to contribute to the support of this great cause, I should state one argument, which impresses my mind forcefully. This is the different kinds of evidence which have been adduced in proof of Christianity, and the confirmation of its truth which results. There is the proof from prophecy, from miracles, from the character of Christ, from that of His apostles, from the nature of Christian doctrines and from the nature and excellence of her practical instructions. There is also the accordance we have pointed out between the doctrine and practice of Christianity, whether considered by themselves or in their mutual relation to each other, and so one could go on. Now, granted that some obscure and illiterate men, residing in a distant province of the Roman empire, had plotted to impose a forgery upon the world, it seems, at least to my understanding, quite impossible that so many different and strong kinds of proof should have come together and united jointly to establish this falsehood.

VI

BRIEF ENQUIRY INTO THE PRESENT STATE OF CHRISTIANITY IN THIS COUNTRY. ITS IMPORTANCE TO US AS A POLITICAL COMMUNITY, AND PRACTICAL HINTS FOR WHICH THE FOREGOING CONSIDERATIONS GIVE OCCASION

Hitherto our discussion has concerned the prevailing religious opinions of professed Christians. But what of the general state of Christianity in this country?

The tendency of religion to promote the temporal well-being of political communities is a fact that is beyond dispute. The peculiar excellence of Christianity in this respect, whether true or false, has been recognised by many writers, who, to say the least, were not disposed to exaggerate its merits. Having admitted either or both of these propositions, the state of religion in a country at any given period, not to mention its connection with the eternal happiness of the inhabitants, becomes immediately a question of great political importance. In particular, it is relevant to ascertain whether religion is advancing or declining. If the latter is the case, then are there any practicable ways of preventing its further decline?

When it is proposed to enquire into the state of religion in any country, and in particular to compare that state with its condition at any former period, there is one preliminary observation that should be made. In every country there exists what may be called a general standard or moral tone, varying in the same community at different periods, and differing at the same period at different levels and situations in society. It follows, of course, that where practice does no more than come up to the accepted level, this will be no confirmation of the existence, much less will it furnish any true measure of the strength, of a true religious faith and practice. Christians, Jews, Turks, infidels, and heretics, persons of ten thousand different sorts of passion and opinion, members at the same time of the same community, and all conscious that they will be examined by this same standard, will regulate their conduct accordingly and adjust themselves to the required measure.

It must also be noted that those things which tend to raise or lower this standard usually produce their effects slowly and almost imperceptibly.

It is a truth which it is difficult to deny, that whenever Christianity has held sway it has raised the general standard of morals to a height before unknown. Some actions, which the ancients scarcely held to be blemishes in the most excellent characters, have been rightly considered by the laws of every Christian community to merit the severest of punishments. In other instances, virtues formerly rare have become common and in particular, a merciful and courteous manner has softened the ruggedness and humanised the brutal ferocity prevalent among the most polished nations of the pagan world. But from what has been observed recently, it is clear that so far as external appearances are concerned, these effects, once Christianity has produced them, are then produced alike in those who deny and in those who admit her divine origins. I almost said in those who reject and in those who accept the Gospel's teaching. These effects would probably remain for a while, without any great change being apparent however her spirit might languish, or her authority decline. When we are enquiring, therefore, into the real state of Christianity at any period, to avoid deception it behoves us to take care and not be taken in by external appearances.

It is a recognised fact that generally persecution tends to invigorate and to propagate the very opinions which she would eradicate. Christianity certainly has always thrived under persecution. At such times she has no lukewarm adherents concerning whom it is dubious to which party they belong. At every turn the Christian is reminded that his Master's kingdom is not of this world. When all on earth is dark and threatening, he looks to heaven for consolation. He considers himself a pilgrim and a stranger. He cleaves then to fundamentals and, as at the hour of death, examines carefully what are his foundations. When religion is surrounded by tranquil calm and prosperity, the contrary of all this applies. The soldiers of the church militant forget that they are in a state of warfare. Their ardour slackens, their zeal languishes. Like a long-standing colony in a strange country, they gradually assimilate its features, demeanour and language and become like native inhabitants. At length, almost every vestige of difference is lost.

If, in general, persecution and prosperity produce opposite effects, this alone might indicate what to expect concerning the state of Christianity in this country, where there has long been an establishment which blends with our civil institutions. It is liberally endowed, has been allowed 'to exalt her mitred front in courts and parliaments'. It is an establishment whose offices are extremely numerous, and these, unlike the Jewish priesthood, filled from a particular race, or the Hindus, held by a separate caste, it is supplied from every class and has ramifications in almost every family in the community. It is also an establishment whose ministers are not, like the Roman Catholic clergy, debarred from marriage, but are allowed so to do; neither are they like some of the more severe religious orders, shut away in colleges and monasteries, but, both by law and custom, they are permitted to mix without restraint in all social activities.

Such being the circumstances of the pastors of the Church, so with the community in general there seems to have been for some time a rapidly improving commercial prosperity. A similar improvement may also be found in the arts and sciences and literary works. It is not difficult to anticipate the effects likely to be produced on true religion, both in the clergy and the laity, by such a state of external prosperity. These effects, inevitably, are favoured when the country in question enjoys a free form of government.

It has been noted by an astute observer that a much looser moral state prevails in the higher than in the middle and lower classes. Now, in every country where the middle classes are growing daily in wealth and importance, and particularly in a country having such a constitution as ours where the acquisition of riches means gaining rank and power, the evils of the upper classes become more widespread and a harmful uniformity of sentiment, manners, and morals diffuses gradually throughout the community. The increasing numbers of large cities and the habit of frequenting a splendid and luxurious metropolis is a powerful influence in spreading the discontinuance of religious habits of a purer age, and in bringing about a more relaxed morality. It has to be admitted that the commercial spirit, much as we are indebted to it, is not conducive to the maintenance of a vigorous and lively state of religion.

In times like these Christianity's strict precepts and self-denying habits naturally fall into disuse and, even among the more committed Christians, they are liable to be softened, so far at least as to be rendered less abhorrent. In such prosperous circumstances, men, in fact, think very little about religion and Christianity seldom occupies the attention of most nominal Christians so that, being rarely the object of their study, they are unacquainted with its tenets. Those doctrines and principles, which it holds in common with the law of the land, or which are sanctioned by the general moral standard, are brought to their notice by the common occurrences of life and therefore might continue to be recognised. But those things which are peculiar to Christianity herself, and which would not be brought to mind by everyday happenings, might be expected to be less and less thought of, till at last they are almost entirely forgotten. Still more so might this be the case, if the features in question were, from their very nature, at war with pride, luxury and worldly-mindedness, which only too frequently go with rapidly increasing wealth. It may also occur that some of the better disposed of the clergy, perhaps from well intentioned though

136

erroneous motives, fail to draw attention in their sermons to this erring way of life.

With so many straying from the right path, from time to time, some bold reformer might not unjustly charge them with their deviation. However, though right in the main, because of his own deviation in an opposite direction, he fails to produce the effect of recalling them from their wanderings.

Still, however, the divine origins of Christianity would not be publicly disavowed, partly from a real and more especially from a political deference for the established faith but, most of all, because most men are not yet prepared to chance their eternal happiness on the question of its being untrue. Some bolder spirits, indeed, might be expected to despise such caution and to pronounce decisively, that the Bible was a forgery. Most people while professing to believe it genuine, would be satisfied to remain ignorant of its contents and when pressed would reveal that they did not believe many of the most important facts contained in it.

When, by these means a country has at last reached such a condition, it is only too obvious that for most of the community, religion, already sunk very low, must rapidly be becoming extinct. Energetic and active causes like these will not suddenly become sluggish and unproductive, but the result is certain and the time is fast approaching when Christianity will be almost as openly disavowed in our language as in fact it is already supposed to have disappeared from men's conduct. Disbelief will then be considered the necessary appendage of a man of fashion and to believe will be deemed to indicate a feeble mind and diminished understanding.

Something along these lines are the conclusions which we should be naturally led to draw concerning the state of Christianity in this country, and its probable termination, from considering its nature, and the peculiar circumstances in which it is placed.

Our hypothetical outline, if correct, will have found approval in the mind of the reader. We can trace everywhere the effects of increasing wealth and luxury, in banishing the habits, and changing the phraseology of stricter times, and in diffusing throughout the middle classes those relaxed morals and dissipated manners, formerly confined to the upper classes of society. Indeed, we do meet with more refinement and more general courtesy, and those evils which are only too common in a ruder and less polished age have become less frequent. These recede on the approach of light and civilisation, but with these excesses, religion, too, has also declined. God is forgotten and His Providence is brought into disrepute. His hand is raised but we do not notice it. He increases our comforts, but we are not grateful. When He chastises us we are not contrite. That part of the week set apart for rest, praise and worship we cheerfully give up to trivia and dissipated living.

But even when religion is not openly and shamelessly disavowed, there are few traces of it to be found. While improving in almost every other branch of knowledge, we have become less and less acquainted with Christianity. This decline of Christianity into a mere system of ethics, may partly be accounted for by considering how our nature has become corrupted, what Christianity is, and the circumstances in which she has been placed in this country. But it has also been promoted in no small way by one peculiar cause, on which it could be helpful to dwell.

In its best days, Christianity (for the benefit of those who consider my statement to be austere and narrow) was indeed as has been outlined in this book. This was the religion of the most eminent reformers, those who suffered martyrdom under Queen Mary and their successors in the times of Elizabeth; in short, of all the pillars of the Protestant Church, including such names as Davenant, Jewell, Hall, Reynolds, Beveridge, Hooker, Andrews, Smith, Leighton, Usher, Hopkins, Baxter, and many others. In their writings, the doctrines peculiar to Christianity were everywhere to be found and on their deep and solid basis were laid the foundations of a broad and high superstructure of morals. Their writings still in existence are proof of this fact and those who lack time, opportunity, or inclination to peruse these may rest assured as they consult our articles and also our liturgy, that such was the Christianity of those times. But because of that tendency to a deterioration in Christian belief, these great fundamental truths became less prominent in the writings of many of the leading divines before the civil wars. During that period, however, the teachings peculiar to Christianity were sadly abused by many who were foremost in the disturbances of those unhappy days. While they talked extensively of Christ's free grace and the operation of the Holy Spirit, by their lives they were an open scandal to the name of Christian.

Towards the end of the eighteenth century, the leaders of the established Church started to run into a different error. They professed it to be their chief object to inculcate the moral and practical precepts of Christianity, without, however, maintaining, or even laying the basis, of a sinner's acceptance by God, or pointing out how Christianity's practical precepts grow out of her peculiar doctrines and are inseparably, connected with them. As a result of this error, the supernatural nature of Christianity imperceptibly underwent a change. She no longer retained her unique character or produced that mental outlook so characteristic of her followers. This example continued to be followed during the present century assisted by various causes already pointed out. In addition to these, for the last fifty years the press has teemed with moral essays, many of them published periodically and circulated extensively. Considered either as mere entertainment, or entertainment blended with instruction, rather than religious pieces, they were kept free from anything that might give them the air of sermons. In this way the fatal habit of considering Christian morality apart from Christian doctrine imperceptibly gained strength. So Christian doctrine was more and more lost to sight and moral standards began to wither and decay. At last today these special doctrines have almost completely vanished. Many sermons even contain scarcely a trace of them.

But the degree to which they are neglected may,

perhaps, be made even more obvious by referring to another criterion. I speak of the writing of novels. A careful examination of the most famous of these works would strongly confirm this fear concerning the very low religious state in this country. But they would still more strikingly illustrate the truth of the remark that the unique features of Christianity have almost been lost to view. In novels, religious people and clergymen, too, are placed in all sorts of situations, and the sentiments and language considered suitable to the occasion is used by them. They are shown as reproving, counselling, or comforting. The author often by intention represents them in a favourable light and accordingly he makes them as well informed and as good Christians as he can. They are painted as amiable, benevolent and forgiving. Yet, without exaggeration, if all Christianity's unique features had never existed, or had been shown to be false, it would hardly be necessary to alter a single syllable of what had been written. It is a striking feature of works by Muslim authors that those characters which they mean to show in a favourable light are made to be far more observant of their religious beliefs and practice.

It is a sad commentary on the direction in which we are moving that many of the most eminent names in literature today are professed unbelievers. Can there then be a doubt as to the direction of the path we travel, and the end to which it must eventually lead us? Take a lesson from experience. In a neighbouring country a similar train of events has occurred with dire consequences. Manners are corrupted, morals depraved, dissipation is rife and, above all, religion is discredited. Unbelief is now the fashion and publicly every religious principle is disavowed. The nation's representatives publicly witness an open, unqualified denial of the very existence of God!

There may be not a few who have witnessed with apprehension and pain the gradual decline in religion, but who at the same time may consider that the present writer tends to go too far. They may even consider that the sort of religion that he aims at is inconsistent with ordinary life and the well-being of society. Were it to prevail generally, people would become wholly engrossed in religion, with all their time occupied by prayer and preaching. Agriculture and commerce would decline, the arts would languish and the ordinary things of life would be neglected.

While there may be some truth in this objection we should not accept the conclusion that is drawn from it. The question remains whether our representation of Christianity's demands agrees with the word of God. For if it does it must surely be admitted to be of small account to sacrifice a little worldly comfort and prosperity, during this short life, in order to secure a crown of eternal glory and the enjoyment of those pleasures which are at God's right hand for everyone! It might be added also, that our Saviour made it clear that Christians would often be required to make such a sacrifice and had forewarned us that, in order to be able to do this, we must sit loose to all our worldly possessions and enjoyments. And it might in addition be pointed out that the widespread prevalence of true Christianity would, far from interfering with national wealth and greatness, turn the world into a scene of general peace and prosperity.

It is true that when Christianity was first proclaimed some of the early converts seem to have been in danger of so far mistaking the principles of the new religion as to imagine that in future they were excused any secular activity or responsibility. But the apostle very pointedly warned them against so gross an error, and expressly and repeatedly advised them to carry out their various duties with greater speed and faithfulness so that they might thereby do credit to the name of Christ. He did this and at the same time emphasised to them the predominance of the love of God and Christ, the heavenly-mindedness, the comparative indifference to the things of this world, the earnest endeavour after growth in grace and perfection in holiness, which are real Christianity's essential characteristics. Remember that the true mark of a Christian is his desire to please God in all his thoughts, words and actions. He takes the revealed word to be the rule of his belief and practice; he aims to let his 'light shine before men' (Matt. 5:16) and in all things to 'make the teaching about God our Saviour

141

attractive' (Titus 2:10). No vocation is proscribed, or pursuit forbidden, no science, art, or pleasure disallowed, which can be reconciled with this principle. However, Christianity does not favour the uncontrolled output of energy and enthusiasm on purely temporal objectives leading to the acquisition of immense wealth or renown. Nor is it designed to gratify the extravagant views of those mistaken politicians whose chief admiration and endeavours for their country are increased dominion, commanding power and unrivalled affluence rather than the more solid advantages of peace, comfort and security. These men would barter comfort for greatness. In their idle dreams they forget that a nation consists of individuals, and that true national prosperity is only the sum of individual happiness.

The fact is that far from real religion producing a stagnation in life, a man, whatever might be his employment or pursuit, will have a new motive to follow it with alacrity, a far more constant and vigorous motive than any human prospects can supply. At the same time, his primary objective not being to succeed but rather to act from a pure principle, and leave the outcome to God, he would not be liable to the same disappointments as those who strive simply for worldly gain or human estimation. So he would possess the true secret of a life which is both useful and happy. Pursuing peace with everyone and regarding them as members of the same family, he would naturally be respected and loved by others, and himself be free from the irritation of those ill feelings which so commonly wear down those who are actuated by worldly principles.

Such would be the happy state within a truly Christian nation. Such a community, peaceable at home, would also be respected and beloved abroad. The general integrity of all its dealings would inspire universal confidence, since differences between nations usually come about because of mutual injuries, jealousy and distrust. But if, in spite of all its justice and restraint, the violence of a neighbouring state forced it to resist an unprovoked attack, strictly defensive hostilities are the only ones in which it would be engaged, its unity at home would double its strength to resist, while the awareness of a good cause and of God's favour lend power to its arm and inspire its efforts.

In spite of what has been said here about the beneficial effects of a Christian society, it has to be admitted that many of the good effects produced by religion would also be produced even by a false religion which prescribed good morals and was able to enforce its precepts by sufficient sanctions. But the superiority of Christianity in this respect must be acknowledged, both in its moral code, and in the powerful motives and effective means supplied to enable us to practise it.

But, above all, this true Christianity, from its essential nature, is peculiarly and powerfully adapted to the preservation and health of political communities. What is in fact their major sickness? The answer is selfishness. This disease is present from birth and it 'grows with their growth, and strengthens with their strength' (Pope). Through it they at last expire. The disease of selfishness assumes different forms in the different classes of society. With the great and wealthy it displays itself in luxury, pomp, parade and in all the frivolities of a sick and depraved mind which seeks in vain its own gratification. It is dead to all the pursuits of a generous heart. In the lower classes, when not weighed down and paralysed by despotism, it shows itself in pride which gives rise to insubordination in all its forms. But though the external effects vary, the internal principle is the same. It is a disposition for all to make themselves the centre and end of all desire and enjoyment. They are disposed to undervalue the advantages and overstate the disadvantages of their position in life. From this state of affairs spring bribery, grasping and licentiousness. The opposite to selfishness is public spirit, which may be termed the underlying principle of political life. It is the very breath of states, which serves to keep them active and vigorous and to carry them to greatness and glory.

The tendency of public spirit, its opposite selfishness, have not escaped the notice of the founders of states, and those who write on government, and various expedients have been resorted to for cherishing the one and repressing the other. Sometimes internal agitation and dissension, resulting from the very structure of the government has produced the effect. Sparta flourished for more than seven hundred years under the civil institutions of Lycurgus. The selfish principle was guarded against by prohibiting commerce and imposing universal poverty and hardship. The Roman commonwealth, in which public spirit was cherished, and selfishness checked by the love of glory, was also of long duration. This passion resulted in an unbounded spirit of conquest, which, like the ambition of the greatest of its own heroes, was never satiated while any other kingdom was left unsubdued. But wealth and luxury produce stagnation, and stagnation terminates in death.

To provide, however, for the continuation of a state by allowing internal dissensions, or even by the influence of poverty, seems to be to sacrifice the end to the means. Happiness is the end for which men unite in civil society; but in societies thus constituted, little happiness is to be found. Again the expedient of preserving a state by the spirit of conquest is not to be tolerated for a moment when considered in terms of universal justice. Such a state lives, grows and thrives by the misery of others, and becomes professedly the general enemy of its neighbours and the scourge of the human race. All these devices are very much man made and compared with the works of the Almighty they are clumsy, weak in operation and full of contradictions and jarring movements. It must be emphasised that Christianity is in every way directly opposed to selfishness, which is the mortal illness of political communities. It might indeed be stated that the main object and concern of Christianity is to eradicate our natural selfishness and to replace its false standard with views which are far higher than any which concern simply our temporal and social well-being. If this brings us to a right estimate of ourselves and of those around us, and to a proper understanding of life's claims and obligations resulting from our various relationships, a general desire to do good is the outcome in the individual's life.

Moderation in temporal activities and pleasures, relative

indifference to the outcome of worldly projects, diligence in the discharge of one's personal and civil duties, resignation to the will of God, and patience with whatever may befall, these are among the daily lessons to be learnt. Humility is one of the essential qualities for doing good. In whatever class or order of society Christianity is to be found, it always works to counteract the particular mode of selfishness, to which that class is liable. Affluence is trained to be liberal and to do good, and authority to operate with meekness, and to be aware of the various cares and responsibilities belonging to its high office. Those in more humble circumstances are also instructed to be diligent, humble and patient. Their more lowly path has been allotted to them by the hand of God and their duty is to be faithful to their posts and contentedly to bear its inconveniences.

The present state of things is very short and the objects over which worldly men strive are not worth the struggle. The peace of mind offered by religion to all indiscriminately affords more true satisfaction than expensive pleasures. In this view the poor have the advantage, and if the rich enjoy more comforts, they are also exposed to many temptations which are peculiar to their position. Most important of all, human distinctions will soon be done away with and the true followers of Christ will all, as children of the same Father, be admitted alike to the possession of the same heavenly inheritance. These are the blessings that Christianity brings to the temporal well-being of political communities.

To produce effects like these Christianity must be real and deep. And this is the religion that we should cultivate in order to bring our speculations to reality and halt the progress of political decay. But in the present state of this country, it is a far greater reason for endeavouring to cultivate this real Christianity, still considering its effects from a purely political standpoint since, humanly speaking, we must either have this or nothing. Unless it can be in some degree restored, we are likely to lose not only all the advantages which we might have derived from true Christianity, but also to incur the manifold evils which the absence of all religion would bring.

In the first place, it should be noted that where religious influence is weak (and even such a one, in a political view, is productive of many advantages), even though its existence is prolonged by favourable circumstances, it can hardly survive when the state of things is so unfavourable as it is in our society today. At one time the religion of the state was generally accepted, though not experienced by all because it was our forefathers' religion. On that account most gave it reverence and admitted its authority without question. In our days, circumstances are very different. The prejudice and respect for former times have abated. Still less will the idea be entertained of maintaining a system for the sake of keeping under the common people. A system, if not supported by a real conviction of its truth, will fall to the ground. Thus it comes about that in a more advanced state of society, a religious establishment is indebted for its support to the religion which it fostered and protected in earlier times, just as a frail and aged mother is sustained, and her life prolonged, by the tender care of the child whom she reared in helpless infancy.

Unless something of that principle which animated our ecclesiastical system in its earlier days is reinfused into our society it is vain to hope that the establishment will continue for very long. The anomaly cannot survive of an establishment, the actual principles of the bulk of whose members and teachers are so extremely different from those which it professes. The kind of religion which we have recommended, whatever opinion may be entertained concerning its truth, and to say nothing of the part played by divine grace, must at least be conceded to be the only one likely to make an impression on the less educated in society. If it is thought that a system of ethics can control the conduct of the upper classes, such a one is altogether unsuitable to the less educated who must be approached through their feelings. The ancients were wiser than we and never thought of governing the community in general by teaching them philosophy. This was confined to the schools for the learned, while for the masses a system of religion was maintained as alone being suitable for their natures.

If in God's mercy, true religion should increase in our society there is no estimating the effect on public morality and our political welfare. These effects are not simply negative, though it would be an achievement purely to check the process which, like gangrene, is destroying the heart of our social and political existence. The general moral standard would be raised and sustained, being kept for a while from further depression. These are all merely natural consequences. But for those who believe in a concerned and caring Providence, it may be added that God's blessing might be on our country, and the effects of His anger, for a while, suspended.

Do not for one moment imagine that our state of civilisation must inevitably guard against moral degeneracy. A neighbouring nation has recently sadly demonstrated that elegant behaviour and refinement can be consistent with a considerable degree of depravity. But to refer to a more emphatic example; in recent years the most celebrated of pagan nations has shown that the highest degree of civilisation and refinement is not inseparable from the most shocking moral depravity. The fact is certain, and the obvious inference with regard to ourselves cannot be denied. The cause of this strange phenomenon has been explained by Paul when writing about most civilised nations of antiquity. 'For although they knew God, they neither glorified him as God nor gave thanks to him . . . since they did not think it worth while to retain the knowledge of God, he gave them over to a depraved mind' (Rom. 1:21–8).

Let us then beware, and take warning from their example. Do not let us allow self-love to lead us astray. Do not imagine that although property and wealth may have caused us to relax a little too much, in those more serious duties which concern our Maker, things will not get any worse, or, at least, that we can never sink into the same state of moral depravation. Doubtless we should sink just as low if God were to give us up also to our own imaginations. And what grounds have we to think that He will not?

147

To argue fairly we should not compare ourselves with the condition of the heathen world at its worst, but with its condition at that time when, because of its forgetfulness of God and its ingratitude towards Him, it was allowed to fall till it reached its ultimate point of depression. The heathen had only reason and natural conscience to direct them. Over and above these we enjoy the clear light of Gospel revelation, and a declaration of God's dealings with them, to warm us. How then can we but believe that if we, who enjoy advantages which are so much superior to theirs, are also forgetful of our generous God, will likewise be left to ourselves? If this is the case why should we not fall into the same crimes?

What then is to be done? This is a question of first importance, and its answer is not difficult. The causes and nature of the decay of religion and morals among us are sufficient to indicate the way which it is expedient that we should go. The illness which ails our community should be seen as a moral rather than a political malady. How often this has been forgotten in present-day arguments on the subject. We should endeavour to retrace our steps. Every effort should be made to raise the level of public morality. All should endeavour to set a good example; something to be followed by the circles in which they move.

It is not only by their personal conduct that those particularly in positions of authority and influence may promote the cause of good morals. By all means let them encourage virtue and discountenance vice in this sphere of influence. Let them enforce the laws by which our forefathers' wisdom has guarded against the grosser breaches of morality, and let them encourage and take part in any plans which may be made in order to advance morality. Above all let them endeavour to instruct and improve the young.

But all attempts will be fruitless to sustain, much less revive, our waning moral standard unless we can also restore the prevalence of evangelical Christianity. As in physics so in morals; unless the original source is raised it will be futile to expect a subsequent flow to be on a high level. All, therefore, who are concerned over our country's welfare, should make every effort to revive the Christianity that we once knew. The attempt should be made especially by the Church's pastors, whose position renders the principles which they hold a matter of supreme importance. Wherever these teachers have steadily and zealously taught true doctrine, the happiest results have often been the outcome and reward. The duty of encouraging true religion in the Church particularly devolves on all who have the disposal of ecclesiastical preferment, and more especially on the Church's dignitaries.

Some of these have already sounded the alarm by rightly censuring the practice of permitting Christianity to degenerate into a mere system of ethics, and recommending more attention to our religion's special doctrines. In our schools and universities the study should be encouraged of the writings of those venerable divines who flourished in the purer times of Christianity. It would be good if a considerable knowledge of their writings was required of candidates for ordination. Let our churches no longer demonstrate that unseemly discord which has existed between the prayers and the sermon that follows.

The above suggestions are seriously submitted to all who have our national welfare at heart. They have been urged, not without misgivings, lest it might appear that eternity's concerns were melted down into a mere matter of temporal advantage or political expediency. But since it has pleased the Almighty so to arrange the constitution of things that the prevalence of true religion and pure morality are conducive to the well-being of states and the preservation of civil order, and since these subordinate inducements are often held out, even by the sacred writers, it seemed right to suggest inferior motives to readers, who might be less disposed to listen to considerations of a higher order.

Would to God that the course of conduct suggested here were properly followed! Would to God also that the happy consequences, resulting from the principles we have recommended could be realised and, above all, that the influence of true religion could be extensively spread abroad! It is the best wish that can be made for his country, by one who is deeply anxious for its welfare.

VII

PRACTICAL HINTS TO VARIOUS DESCRIPTIONS OF PERSONS

Section I

So we have tried to trace the chief defects in religious practice found in most professing Christians in this country. We have pointed out their low estimate of the importance of Christianity in general, their inadequate conceptions of its leading doctrines and the natural result of relaxing the strictness of its practice. Above all, we have noted their misconception of its unique nature. Do not let the difference between them and true believers be considered of minor degree, a matter of forms or opinions. The question is of the very stuff of religion. The difference is most serious and momentous in degree. We must speak out. Their Christianity is not Christianity. It lacks the essential principle and it is deficient in all the important constituents. Let them be deceived no longer by names in so important a matter, but with humble prayer to the giver of all wisdom for an enlightened understanding, and a heart clear of prejudice, let them seriously examine by the standard of Scripture their belief and practice. They will then become aware of just how shallow it is.

If by God's blessing on anything written here there should be any who feels the urge to self-examination, let me first warn them to be well aware of our natural proneness to see ourselves in too favourable a light. Selfishness is one of the principal fruits of the corruption of human nature and it disposes us to overrate our good qualities and to overlook or exercise our defects. The corruption of human nature being what it is, if we would form a just estimate of our character, we must make allowance of the effects of selfishness. Another effect of the corruption of human nature is to cloud our moral sight and blunt our moral sensibility. Allowance must therefore be made for this also. Doubtless God's perfect purity enables Him to see in us stains, far more in number and deeper in dye than we ourselves can discover.

Nor should we forget that when we look into ourselves only those sins which we have recently committed are likely to make any deep impression. Many individual sinful acts or a continued course of vicious or dissipated behaviour, which when recent may have smitten us with deep remorse, after a few months or years leave very little trace in our memory. But it is those strong impressions which they first excited that provide the true measure of their guilt. To the pure eyes of God, that guilt must always have appeared far greater than to us. Now with God there is no past or future, so that all is retained by Him in present and unvarying contemplation, continuing always to appear just the same as at the first moment of its happening. Well may we then humble ourselves in the sight of the one whose 'eyes are too pure to look on evil' (Hab. 1:13), to behold and remember that unless our offences have been blotted out through true repentance and a living faith in Christ, we appear in His eyes as clothed with the sins of our whole lives, in all their original depth of colour and with all the aggravating features which we no longer remember in detail, though they once filled us with confusion and shame.

The writer is concerned to emphasise this approach since he has found no more efficacious way of producing in his own mind the deepest humiliation.

In discussing the sources of the erroneous ideas we hold about our religious and moral character, it may be helpful to point out some other common ways of self-deception. Many people are misled by others' favourable opinions of them. Many mistake a fervent zeal for orthodoxy for the acceptance of Gospel truths. And almost all of us, from time to time, confuse the suggestions of the understanding with the impulses of the will, the assent which our judgment

151

gives to religious and moral truths, with a hearty belief and approval of them.

There is another frequent source of self-deception, capable of producing harm, that must be mentioned. To understand better let it be assumed that certain evil, and also certain good deeds, seem naturally to belong to certain periods and conditions of life. Now, if we should argue fairly when we estimate our moral character, we ought to examine ourselves with reference to that particular sin which besets us and not to some other sin to which we are not so liable. And similarly we ought not to be complacent if we find in ourselves that good and amiable quality which comes naturally to us at this time or condition. Rather we should look for some less ambiguous evidence of genuine virtue. But we are prone to reverse these rules of judging, and both in ourselves and in others we excuse the besetting sin, taking and giving credit for being exempt from those to which we or they are less liable. On the other hand, we give ourselves credit for the possession of a good or amiable quality which is ours by nature and look for no more satisfactory evidence of the adequacy of our moral character. The bad effects of such partiality are made worse by the practice, to which we are prone, of being satisfied, when we take a hurried view of ourselves, with negative evidences of our condition. We think all is well if we are not shocked by some great wrong deed instead of looking for the positive evidences of a true Christian, as outlined in Scripture.

But the source of self-deception is our tendency to consider it a conquest of particular vice when in fact we have merely left the period or condition of life to which that event belongs. At this stage we may substitute for it an evil peculiar to the new period or condition on which we are entering. So we mistake outgrowing or relinquishing our vices, from some change in our worldly circumstances, for a thorough reformation. But this topic deserves to be looked at a little more closely. Young people can be inconsiderate and dissipated. The youth of one sex may indulge occasionally in licentious excesses, while those of the other may be given up to vanity and pleasure. Provided, however, they are sweet tempered and open, and not disobedient to their parents or other superiors, the former are deemed good-hearted young men, the latter, innocent young women. Those who love them best have no concern for their spiritual interests and they would be considered oddly strict in themselves (or in others) were they to doubt that they would become more religious as they grew older; or to speak of them as being actually under divine displeasure; or to entertain any apprehensions concerning their future destiny.

They grow older, and marry. The same licentiousness, which was formerly considered in young men as an excusable weakness, is now no longer regarded in the husband and the father as compatible with the character of a decently religious man. The language goes like this: 'They have sown their wild oats, they must now reform and be regular.' Similarly the matron, for she is kind in her conjugal and parental relations, she is decent in her behaviour and acceptable in society as a good sort. In spite of this, their hearts are no more than before concerned over the great work of their salvation, but are bent on increasing their fortunes, or raising their families. They congratulate themselves, meanwhile, on having given up those sins they are no longer strongly tempted to commit, or whose commission would prejudice their characters and perhaps injure their fortune in life.

Old age has at last arrived. Now, if ever, we might expect that it would be considered high time to make eternal things the main object of attention. No such thing! There is still an appropriate good quality, the presence of which calms the unease and satisfies the demands both of themselves and of those around them. They are now required to be good-natured and cheerful, indulgent to the frailties and follies of the young, remembering that when young themselves they gave in to the same practices. How different this is to that dread of sin, which is the mark of a true Christian! It causes him to look back upon the sins of his own youthful days with shame and sorrow, and instead of conceding that for young people to be wild and thoughtless is a privilege belonging to their age and circumstances, it prompts him to warn them against what has proved to him a matter of such bitter retrospection! So he is found to stifle the voice of conscience. We cry peace 'when there is no peace' (Jer. 6:14) and both on us and others a complacency descends which ought only to proceed from a consciousness of being reconciled to God, and a humble hope of our possessing His favour.

These will be considered uncharitable thoughts; but we must not let this deter us. It is time to have done with senseless charitable cant which insults the understanding and trifles with the feelings of those who are really concerned for the happiness of their fellow-creatures. Charity is partial to the object of her regard and where actions are of a doubtful quality, this disposes her to assume a good rather than a bad motive. She is also apt to exaggerate merits and to see amiable qualities in a more favourable light than that which strictly belongs to them. But true charity is alert, fervent, full of concern and good deeds, not easily satisfied and not prepared to believe that everything is going on well as a matter of course. But she is apprehensive of harm, quick to suspect danger and prompt to extend relief. These are the ways in which genuine regard will show itself in a wife or mother in the case of the bodily health of the object of her affections. And where there is any real concern for the spiritual interests of others, it is characterised by the same infallible marks. The wretched quality, by which the name of charity is now so generally and falsely usurped, is no other than indifference. Against the plainest evidence, or at least strong ground for apprehension, it is content to believe that all is well, because it has no anxieties to allay, or fears to repress. It experiences no change of feeling. It is not at one moment flushed with hope, or at another chilled by disappointment.

To a considerate and feeling mind, there is something very distressing to see the engaging cheerfulness and cloudless gaiety of youth accepted as a sufficient evidence of inner purity by delighted parents who, knowing the deceitfulness of these flattering appearances, should make good use of this time, once lost never to be regained, of good-humoured acquiescence and docility. It is a period when the soft and malleable nature of the mind renders it more susceptible to impressions. A time, therefore, when habits should be formed, which may assist our natural weakness in resisting the temptations to which we shall be exposed in later life. This applies especially to the female sex, because that sex seems to be more favourably disposed than ours to the feelings and practices of religion; and have been fitted by God's mercy to carry out the important task of the education of young children. Doubtless, this more favourable disposition to religion in the female sex is doubly valuable in the wedded state and it seems to afford to the married man the way of rendering an active business life more compatible with devotional feelings.

When the husband returns to his family, worn and harassed by worldly cares or professional duties, the wife, regularly keeping a warmer and more unimpaired spirit of devotion than is perhaps consistent with immersion in the bustle of life, is in a position to revive his inert piety, and so the religious experience of both gains new force and tenderness from mutual conjugal affection. Can a more pleasing picture be drawn than that of a couple, happy in each other and in the pledges of their mutual love, uniting in an act of grateful adoration to the author of all their mercies. They recommend each other and the objects of their common care to God's protection and repress the concerns of conjugal and parental tenderness by a confident hope, that through all the changes of this uncertain life, the disposer of all things will certainly cause everything to work together for the good of them that love and put their trust in Him.

After this uncertain state has passed away, they know that they will be admitted to a joint participation in never-ending happiness. It is surely no mean or ignoble office which we allot to the female sex, when in this way we commit to them the charge of exercising whatever emotions most dignify and adorn human nature and when we would make them, as it were, the medium of our intercourse with the heavenly world, the faithful repositories of the religious

155

belief for the benefit both of the present and of the rising generation. Must it not then excite our grief and indignation, when we see mothers who are forgetful both of their own special duties and of the high office which God designed that they should fulfil?

Innocent young women! Good-hearted young men! Wherein does this goodness of heart and innocence lie? Remember that we are fallen creatures, born in sin, and naturally depraved. Christianity does not recognise innocence or goodness of heart, apart from the remission of sin and the effects of the operation of God's grace. Do we find in these young persons the characters, which Scripture lays down as the satisfactory evidence of a safe state? Do we not, rather, find the specific marks of a state of alienation from God? Can any persuade themselves that they are loving, or striving to love God with all their hearts and souls and minds (Matt. 22:37)? Are they seeking 'first his kingdom and his righteousness' (Matt. 6:33)? Are they working out their 'salvation with fear and trembling' (Phil. 2:12)? Are they clothed 'with humility' (1 Pet. 5:5)? Are they not, rather, given up to self-indulgence? Are they not at least 'lovers of pleasure rather than lovers of God' (2 Tim. 3:4)? Is religious observance a solace or a task? Do they not come reluctantly to these services, continue in them by constraint, and quit them gladly? And how many of these persons may it not be affirmed in the spirit of the prophet's language: 'They have harps and lyres at their banquets, tambourines and flutes and wine, but they have no regard for the deeds of the Lord, no respect for the work of his hands' (Isa. 5:12)?

Are not the youth of one sex committing, or wishing for the opportunity to commit, those sins which Scripture says expressly, 'those who live like this will not inherit the kingdom of God' (Gal. 5:21)? Once the ebullience of youth is passed they may be decent, sober, useful, respectable members of the community, or pleasant in domestic relations. But is this the change Scripture speaks about? Listen to the expressions which it uses, and judge for yourselves. 'Except a man is born again, he cannot see the kingdom of God' (John 3:3 AV). '. . . your old self, which is being corrupted by its deceitful desires' (Eph. 4:22), an expression but too descriptive of the vain delirium of youthful dissipation and the false dreams of pleasure which it inspires. But 'the new self' awakened from this false estimate of happiness 'is being renewed in knowledge in the image of its Creator' (Col. 3:10). He is 'created to be like God in true righteousness and holiness' (Eph. 4:24). The persons of whom we are speaking are indeed no longer so thoughtless, wild and dissipated as they were, so negligent in their attention to objects of real value, so eager in the pursuit of pleasure or so prone to yield to the impulse of appetite. But this is no more than the change that belongs naturally to their riper years.

Another way of tackling this question is by regarding life as a state of probation. Probation implies resisting, in obedience to the dictates of religion, appetites which by nature we are prompted to gratify. Young people are not tempted to be churlish, interested and covetous, but to be inconsiderate and dissipated, 'lovers of pleasure rather than lovers of God.' (2 Tim. 3:4). In middle age people are not tempted so strongly to be thoughtless and idle and licentious, for they are sufficiently withheld from excesses of this sort, particularly when happily settled in domestic life, or for the sake of their good name, by the restraints of family connections, and by a sense of what is owed to the decencies of the married state. Their probation is of another sort. They are tempted to be supremely engrossed by worldly cares, family interests, professional objects, the pursuit of wealth or of ambition. Thus occupied, 'Their mind is on earthly things' (Phil. 3:19), and they forget that 'only one thing is needed' (Luke 10:42). They set their minds on temporal rather than eternal concerns, and take up with 'a form of godliness' (2 Tim. 3:5), instead of seeking to experience its power.

The foundations of this nominal religion are laid, as was formerly explained, in the forgetfulness, if not in the ignorance, of Christianity's special peculiar doctrines. These are the ready-made Christians formerly mentioned who consider Christianity as a geographical term, properly applicable to all those who have been born and educated in a country wherein Christianity is professed and not as indicating a new nature, expressing a unique character, with its appropriate desires, aversions, hopes, fears, joys and sorrows. To these people Christ's solemn admonition is addressed: 'I know your deeds; you have a reputation of being alive, but you are dead. Wake up! Strengthen what remains and is about to die, for I have not found your deeds complete in the sight of my God' (Rev. 3:1–2).

If anyone is inclined to listen to this solemn warning, having been wakened from his dream of false security, and is desirous to be not only almost but altogether a Christian – let him not stifle or dispel these beginnings of religious concern, but diligently cherish them as the work of the Holy Spirit, which would draw him from the broad and crowded road of destruction into the narrow and thinly peopled path 'that leads to life' (Matt. 7:14). Let him leave the crowd, enter into his closet, and on bended knees implore for Christ's sake and in reliance on His mediation, that God will remove from him the 'heart of stone, and give . . . a heart of flesh' (Ezek. 11:19), that the Father of light would open his eyes to his true condition, and take from his heart the clouds of prejudice and dissipate all self-love. Next let him examine carefully his past life and his present course of conduct, comparing himself with God's word: and considering how anyone might reasonably have been expected to behave when the Holy Scriptures had been always available, and he had admitted them to be the revelation of the will of his Creator, God. Let him there peruse the awful denunciations against impenitent sinners and strive to become more and more deeply impressed with a realisation of his own radical blindness and corruption. Above all, let him contemplate steadily every aspect of that stupendous truth, the incarnation and crucifixion of the only begotten Son of God, and the message of mercy proclaimed from the cross to repenting sinners. 'Be reconciled to God' (2 Cor. 5:20). 'Believe in the Lord Jesus, and you will be saved' (Acts 16:31).

When he estimates the guilt of his sin by the payment which was required to atone for it, and the value of his soul by the price which was paid for its redemption, and contrasts both of these with his own stupid lack of consideration, when, too, he reflects on the amazing love and pity of Christ and on his own cold and formal acknowledgment of it, making light of the precious blood of the Son of God, and trifling with the gracious invitations of his Redeemer, surely, mixed emotions of guilt, fear, shame, remorse and sorrow will overwhelm his soul. Smiting his breast, he will cry out in the words of the publican, 'God, have mercy on me, a sinner' (Luke 18:13). But, thank God, such a one does not need to despair. It is to such that the offers of the Gospel are proffered and its promises assured; to the 'weary and burdened' (Matt. 11:28) under the weight of their sins; to those who thirst for the water of life; to those who feel themselves tied and bound by the chain of their sins, who abhor their captivity and earnestly long for deliverance. Happy those souls whom God in His grace has visited, 'has rescued' from the dominion of darkness . . . 'into the kingdom of the Son he loves' (Col. 1:13). Cast yourselves, then, on His undeserved mercy, for He is full of love, and will not spurn you. Surrender into His hands, and resolve solemnly through His grace, to dedicate henceforth all your faculties and powers to His service.

It is for you now 'to work out your salvation with fear and trembling', relying on the faithfulness of Him who has promised to work 'in you to will and to act according to his good purpose' (Phil. 2:12–13). Always look to Him for help. Your only safety consists in a deep and abiding sense of your own weakness, and in a firm reliance on His strength. You are enlisted under the banner of Christ. Fear not, though the world, the flesh and the devil are set in array against you. '. . . he who promised is faithful' (Heb. 10:23). 'Be faithful, even to the point of death, and I will give you the crown of life' (Rev. 2:10). '. . . he who stands firm to the end will be saved' (Matt. 10:22).

In the present world you must be prepared to meet with many difficulties. Arm yourselves, therefore, in the first place with a firm resolution not to overrate human estimation, not to fear the charge of being exclusive, when it is necessary to incur it, but make it your constant endeavour to keep in your mind's eye, that bright assembly of invisible spectators who are the witnesses of your daily conduct and to seek 'the praise that comes from the only God' (John 5:44). You cannot advance a single step till you possess this relative indifference to men's favour. As we have already commented no one should needlessly go out of his way to be different. But to attempt to combine two incompatibles, to seek to please God and the world, where their commands are really at variance, is the way to be neither respectable, good, nor happy. Remain always aware of your own basic corruption and weakness. Indeed, if your eyes are really opened, and your heart truly softened, you will become daily more and more aware of your own defects, needs and weaknesses, and more and more impressed by a feeling of the mercy and long-suffering of our gracious Saviour, who 'forgives all your sins, and heals all your diseases' (Ps. 103:3).

This is the solution of what to a man of the world might seem a strange paradox, that in proportion as the Christian grows in grace, he grows also in humility. Humility is indeed the essential principle of Christianity. The principle whereby she lives and thrives, and in proportion to the growth or decline of which she must flourish or decay. This first disposes the penitent sinner to accept the offers of the Gospel and during his whole progress this is the ground and basis of his feelings and conduct, both in relation to God, his fellow-creatures and himself. When at length he shall be translated into the realms of glory, this principle will still remain in undiminished force for he will fall down; and cast his crown before the Lamb; and saying 'Blessing, and honour, and glory, and power, be unto him that sitteth upon the throne, and unto the Lamb for ever and ever' (Rev. 5:13 AV).

The practical benefits which spring from a habitual lowliness of spirit are numerous. It will lead you to dread sin's onset and to fly from sinful activity as a man would avoid some infectious illness. It will prevent a thousand difficulties, and decide a thousand questions concerning worldly involvement; embarrass those who are not aware of their personal frailty, whose view of Christian character is not sufficiently high and who are not enough continually possessed with a fear that they might 'grieve the Holy Spirit of God' (Eph. 4:30) and so provoke Him to withdraw His gracious influence. But if you are really such as we have been describing, there is no need to urge you to set a high standard of practice and to strive after universal holiness. It is your heart's desire to act with a single eye in all things to God's favour and so the most ordinary actions of life will become acts of worship. Because of our desire to please God we should be always careful to discover the path of duty. We should not just wait indolently, finding it sufficient not to refuse occasions to glorify God when they are forced upon us. Rather we should pray to God for wisdom and spiritual understanding, that we may be vigilant in seeing opportunities to serve Him in the world.

Do guard against the distraction of worldly care and cultivate heavenly-mindedness with a spirit of continual prayer. Do not forget to watch incessantly over the workings of your deceitful heart, but at the same time be active and useful. Do not let your precious times be wasted 'in shapeless idleness'; an admonition which today is made only too necessary by the relaxed habits of even religious people. Never be satisfied with your present attainments, but 'Forgetting what is behind, strain towards what is ahead' (Phil. 3:13) with undiminished energy, and to run the race that is set out for you without flagging in your course.

Above all, measure your progress by the improvement in your love for God and man. 'God is love' (1 John 4:8) is the sacred principle which warms and enlightens the heavenly world where God dwells. There it shines with unclouded radiance. Some scattered beams are graciously lent to us on earth, but a larger portion of it is infused into the hearts of God's servants who in this way are renewed in God's likeness and even here may show some faint traces of the image of their heavenly Father. It is the principle of love which disposes them to yield themselves without reserve to the service of Him who has bought them with the price of His own blood.

Most nominal Christians regard these ideas of Christian practice to be servile, base and mercenary. They give no more than they dare not withhold and abstain from nothing but what they must not practise. In short, they know Christianity only as a system of restraints. But true Christians do not see themselves as satisfying some rigorous creditor, but as discharging a debt of gratitude. Theirs is not the stinted return of a constrained obedience, but the large and generous measure of a voluntary service. This principle regulates the true Christian's choice of companions and friends, where he is at liberty to express an option. It fills him with the wish to promote the good of all around him and still more, with pity, love and anxious concern for their spiritual welfare. Indifference, indeed, in this respect is one of the surest signs of a low or declining state of spirituality. This life-giving principle in the true Christian's happier hour inspires his devotions, and makes him delight in the worship of God. This fills him with consolation, peace and gladness, and sometimes even enables him to be filled with 'an inexpressible and glorious joy' (1 Pet. 1:8).

But this world is not his resting place. Here, to the very last, he must be a pilgrim and a stranger. He is a soldier, whose warfare ends only with life, ever struggling and combatting with the powers of darkness, the temptations of the world around him and the still more dangerous hostilities of internal depravity. The constant changes, the peculiar trials and difficulties which chequer the life of a Christian and still more, the painful and humiliating memory of his own weaknesses teach him to look forward to that promised day, when he shall be completely delivered from the bondage of corruption and sorrow and sighing shall flee away. In anticipation of that blessed state and comparing this churlish turbulent world of competition, envy, anger and revenge with that blissful place where love shall reign undisturbed, the true Christian triumphs over the fear of death. He longs for the realisation of these cheering visions and to join that blessed company.

What has been said about the habitual feelings of the true believer may suggest a reply to the objection commonly expressed by nominal Christians, that we should deny men life's innocent amusements and gratifications. In this way our religion assumes a gloomy forbidding aspect, instead of the true and natural aspect of cheerfulness and joy.

In the first place, religion does not prohibit innocent amusement or gratification. The question of its innocence, however, must not be tried by the loose standards of worldly morality, but by the spirit of the injunctions of the word of God and by the activity being conformable to thought and action. There can be no dispute concerning recreation's true end. It is intended to refresh our exhausted bodily or mental powers, and to restore us, with renewed vigour, to the more serious occupations of life. Whatever, therefore, fatigues rather than refreshes the body or mind, does not answer the designed purpose. Whatever consumes more time, money or thought than is necessary to allot to mere amusement, can hardly be approved by anyone who considers time as something for which he will have to give account. Also whatever is likely to injure the welfare of a fellow-creature can scarcely be a suitable or consistent recreation for a Christian, who is told 'love your neighbour as yourself' (Matt. 19:19).

But does a Christian never relax? Let us not so wrong and vilify Providence's bounty as to admit for a moment that the forms of innocent amusement are so few that men are forced to indulge in those of a doubtful quality. No! There are many and varied means of innocent recreation. The Christian relaxes in the temperate use of all of God's gifts. Imagination, taste, genius, the beauties of creation and works of art are all open for him. He relaxes in good conversation, in social intercourse, in the sweetness of friendship, the endearments of love, the exercise of hope, confidence, joy, gratitude, universal goodwill and all the benevolent and generous emotions. By the gracious ordination of our Creator, while these intend only happiness to others,

163

they are productive of peace and relaxation to ourselves. Little do these know of the true measure of enjoyment, who can compare these tranquil pleasures with the frivolous ones of dissipation, or sensuality's coarse gratifications.

It is no wonder, however, that the nominal Christian should give up reluctantly, one by one, the pleasures of the world, and look back upon them with wistful and regretful eyes. He does not know the sweetness of the delights which true Christianity repays for those trifling sacrifices. It is true that when anyone who has led a life of gross and unrestrained evil is checked in his career and commences the Christian life, he has many changes to experience. Fear, guilt, remorse, shame and various other passions struggle and conflict within him. Appetites clamour for their accustomed gratification, and old habits are hard to resist. They are weighed down by a load of guilt, and almost overwhelmed by a sense of unworthiness. But all this should really be charged to the account of their past sins and not to that of their present repentance. This state of suffering rarely continues very long. When mental gloom is at its blackest, a ray of heavenly light occasionally breaks in and suggests the hope of better days.

When we maintain that the ways of religion are pleasant we do not mean to deny that the Christian is himself always in a state of discipline and warfare. It must be admitted that a little religion is apt to make men gloomy. Hence the unjust imputation often brought upon religion by those whose degree of religion is just sufficient, by condemning their course of conduct, to render them uneasy. It is enough merely to impair the sweetness of the pleasures of sin, and not enough for its own special comforts to compensate for the relinquishment of them. Thus these men give a negative and unattractive account of our promised land, which in fact abounds with all that we can require in our journey through life.

There are, of course, other sources of pleasure for the Christian which men of the world cannot understand. Quite apart from a degree of exemption from distracting passions and corroding cares which harass the non-Christian, there is the peace and hope that come from being reconciled to God and enjoying His favour. There is that solid peace of mind which the world can neither give nor take away, and which results from a firm confidence in God's infinite wisdom and goodness and in the unceasing care and kindness of our Saviour. And there is the divine assurance that all things will work together for good.

In youth, health and vigour when all goes prosperously and success abounds, we do not feel the need of the consolations of religion. When fortune frowns, however, or friends forsake, when sorrow, sickness or old age comes upon us, at these times the superiority of the pleasures of religion is established over those of dissipation and futility. There is scarcely a more melancholy sight than that of an old man who is a stranger to the only true source of satisfaction. How sad it is to see such a one, awkwardly grasping for the pleasures of his younger years, which are now beyond his reach, or feebly attempting to hold on to them, while they mock his endeavours and elude his grasp! To such a one, gloomily indeed does the evening of life set in! All is sour and cheerless. He can neither look backward with complacency, nor forward with hope. The aged Christian, however, relying on his Redeemer's assured mercy, can calmly reflect that his end is at hand and his redemption draws near. As his strength declines, and his faculties decay, he can quietly repose himself on God's faithfulness and at the very entrance of the valley of the shadow of death, he can lift up an eye, dim, perhaps, and feeble, yet sparkling with hope, and confidently looking forward to soon possessing his heavenly inheritance, the joys of which, 'No eye has seen, no ear has heard, no mind has conceived' (1 Cor. 2:9).

Never were there times than those in which we live, which impressed more forcibly the wisdom of seeking happiness which is beyond the reach of human fortunes. Wealth, power and prosperity, how peculiarly transitory and uncertain they are! The superiority of the support derived from religion is felt less when the Christian is in full possession of riches, splendour, rank and all the gifts of nature and fortune. But when all these are swept away by time's rough hand, or the blasts of adversity, the true Christian stands, like the glory of the forest, erect and vigorous. He is stripped indeed of his summer foliage, but more than ever finding for himself the solid strength of his substantial fabric.

Section II
Advice to some who profess full assent to the fundamental doctrines of the Gospel

In an early chapter we enlarged on what may be termed the fundamental practical error of most professed Christians today. They either overlook or misconceive the special method provided by the Gospel for the renovation of our corrupt nature, and for attaining every Christian grace.

But there are mistakes made on both sides. Our proneness, when going from one extreme is to run into an opposite error, and this makes it necessary for us to add another admonition. The generally prevailing error today is the fundamental one which was formerly pointed out. But while we attend to this, and on the instruction both of Scripture and experience, advise heartfelt repentance and true faith as the only roots and foundations of true holiness, we must at the same time guard against a practical mistake of another kind. Those who, with penitent hearts, have humbled themselves before the cross of Christ, pleaded His merits as their only ground of pardon and acceptance and resolved henceforth, through the help of the Holy Spirit, to produce the fruits of righteousness, are sometimes apt to behave as if they considered that their work was complete. If they should happen to fall into more sin, then a further act of repentance and faith would be called for.

There are not a few in our relaxed age who satisfy themselves with what may be termed general Christianity. They feel general penitence and humiliation as a result of their general sinfulness, and a desire for universal holiness, but they neglect that vigilance and apprehension with which they should work to eradicate every form of corruption from their being. Similarly, they are far from striving with persevering readiness to acquire and improve on every Christian grace. Nor is it unusual for ministers, who faithfully, ably and successfully preach the Gospel truths to be themselves liable to the charge of concentrating in their instructions on this general religion. Rather they should be tracing and laying bare the secrets of inward corruption, and instructing their hearers how best to conduct themselves in every area of Christian warfare and the best way to battle with each particular evil and to cultivate each grace of the Christian character.

In too many persons, concerning the sincerity of whose general religious professions we should be sorry to entertain a doubt, we see little progress being made in the control of their tempers, the improvement of their time, the reform of their way of life, or ability to resist the temptation to which they are particularly exposed. They will admit that they are 'miserable sinners'; this is a tenet of their creed and they even feel proud of admitting it. They will occasionally also admit to particular failings, but this confession is sometimes made in order to cause a compliment to be made on the very opposite virtue. Where this is not the case, it is often not difficult to detect under this guise of false contrition, a secret self-satisfaction arising from the now general knowledge of their acuteness or candour in revealing the weakness in question, or of their frankness or humility in acknowledging it. Anyone who either watches the workings of his own heart, or observes that the faults confessed in these instances are very seldom the person's worst offences, will agree that this is not an unjust assessment.

We must warn these men and their instructors plainly, that they are in danger of deceiving themselves. These persons need to be reminded that there is no short cut to holiness. It must be the business of their whole lives to grow in grace, and continually to add one virtue to another and as far as is possible 'go on to maturity' (Heb. 6:1). 'He who does what is right is righteous' (1 John 3:7). Unless they are producing evidence of the fruit of the Spirit in their lives there is no certainty that they have received the Spirit of

Christ, without which they do not belong to Him. But even if we entertain the hope that they in fact are true believers, nevertheless we must tell them that they are not acting in a manner which is glorifying to Christ. The world does not see their private devotions, but it is quick to notice any faults in their way of life. If it sees that they have the same eagerness, the same ungoverned tempers, which are found in people in general, it will treat with contempt their pretences to sanctity and indifference to worldly things. And its prejudices will be hardened against the only means which God has provided for us to escape the wrath to come and to obtain eternal happiness.

Let him, then, who would indeed be a Christian, keep a close watch on his ways and heart. Let him attempt to learn from men and books and particularly from the lives of eminent Christians, the best ways to overcome temptation and to grow in every aspect of holiness. So by studying his own character, and observing the innermost recesses of his own mind, the knowledge which he will acquire of the human heart in general, and especially of his own, will be of the highest help to him in avoiding or guarding against the temptations to sin. It is by this unceasing diligence, as the apostle declares, that the servants of Christ must make their calling sure.

Section III
Brief observations addressed to sceptics and Unitarians

There is another class of people, sadly increasing in number in this country, that of the absolute unbelievers to whom this little book has not been primarily directed. The writer, pitying sinners their melancholy state, would like to ask them one plain question. If Christianity is not in their estimation true, is there not at least a sufficiency in its favour to entitle it to be examined seriously? It has after all been accepted not blindly and implicitly but after full enquiry and deep consideration, by Bacon, Milton, Locke and Newton, and the majority of those, who, by the

168

breadth of their understandings, the extent of their knowledge, the freedom of their minds, and their daring to combat existing prejudices, have invoked the respect and admiration of mankind. It might be considered scarcely fair to instance clergymen, though some of them are among the greatest names this country has ever known. Can the sceptic honestly say that he has made a thorough examination into the evidence of revelation at all, or at least with a seriousness and diligence in any degree proportionate to the importance of the subject? The fact is that unbelief is not the outcome of genuine enquiry. It is rather the result of a careless, irreligious life, combined with prejudices and erroneous conceptions concerning the nature of the leading doctrines and fundamental beliefs of Christianity.

Take the case of young people brought up as nominal Christians. When children, they are taken to church, and become acquainted with those parts of Scripture contained in the services. If their parents still more adhere to the customs of better times, they are taught their catechism and a little more religious knowledge. After a while, they leave the supervision of their parents and they enter into the world and follow some career or other. They yield to the temptations which come at them, and become more or less dissipated and licentious. They give up reading the Bible. They do not find other ways to increase their religious knowledge. They do not even try, by reflection and study, to make their own those opinions which, in their childhood, they had to take on trust. They travel, perhaps abroad, a process which tends naturally to weaken their childhood prejudice in favour of the religion in which they were brought up and because it removes them from all means of public worship, they become lax in religious habits. They return home, and commonly are either rushed round in a whirl of dissipation, or engage with youthful ardour in some public or professional pursuit. If they read or hear anything about Christianity, it is usually those parts which are the subject of controversy and what they hear from the Bible, in their occasional attendance at church, while it may sometimes impress them with an idea of the purity of

169

Christian morality, contains much which, coming in this detached way, perplexes and offends them.

Various doubts and objections arise which a further acquaintance with the Scripture would remove. So growing more and more to know Christianity only by its difficulties and sometimes tempted by an ambition to show themselves superior to what they think to be vulgar prejudice, also disgusted possibly by the immoral lives of some professed Christians, all encourages many doubts and suspicions to spring up within them. These doubts enter into the mind almost imperceptibly at first and exist only as vague indistinct surmises. They by no means take the precise shape or substance of a formed opinion. At first they may even offend and startle by their intrusion, but by degrees the unpleasant sensations they once excited wear off and the mind grows more familiar with them. The impression becomes deeper and at last they diffuse themselves over the whole of religion, and hold total sway in the whole mind.

While not universal, this might be termed, perhaps not unjustly, the natural history of scepticism. It fits in with the experience of those who have carefully watched the progress of unbelief in the people around them. It is confirmed by the autobiographies of some of the most eminent unbelievers. It is curious to read their own accounts of themselves which accord so exactly with what we have noted. Once, perhaps, they gave a sort of implicit hereditary assent to Christian truth and were what the world would term believers. What woke them from their sleep of ignorance? When did the light of truth shine on them and scatter the darkness which enveloped them? The time of their unbelief is not marked by any definite boundary. Reason, thought and enquiry had little or nothing to do with it. Having for many years lived careless and irreligious lives, and associated with companions of similar outlook, it was not because of study and meditation, but rather the passage of time that brought their unbelief to maturity. It is worth noting that where they are reclaimed from unbelief it is usually by a process much more rational than that which has been here described. Something awakens them to reflection. They examine, consider and at last yield their assent to Christianity on what they consider to be sufficient grounds.

From this account here given it is apparent that unbelief usually springs from prejudice and that it succeeds mainly because of human depravity. Unbelief spreads in proportion to the decline in public morality. To any fair mind this argument alone should suffice in deciding against unbelief and in favour of revelation. Those who favour Christianity might, with justification, return their opponent's charge, made with the affectation of superior wisdom, that we surrender ourselves implicitly instead of examining dispassionately the ground of our faith and only yielding our assent according to the weight of evidence.

Unbelief increases today not as a result of study of the writings of unbelievers, but from the increase in luxury and the decay in morality. Where the words of sceptical writers have been to blame it has been produced not by argument and discussion but by sarcasm and points of wit, operating on weak minds, or on nominal Christians by gradually bringing into contempt opinions which for them had rested only on the basis of blind respect and the prejudices of education. It is therefore axiomatic that unbelief is in general a disease of the heart rather than the understanding. If revelation were assailed only by reason and argument, it would have little to fear. The literary opposers of Christianity, from Herbert to Hume, have been seldom read. They made some stir in their day when for a brief span, they were noisy and noxious, but like locusts which for a while obscure the air and destroy the vegetation they were soon swept away and forgotten.

In the course which we traced from nominal orthodoxy to absolute unbelief, Unitarianism is a sort of halfway house. The Unitarian teachers do not absolve their followers from strict Christian morality. They lay down the all importance of the love of God and a constant spirit of devotion. But it is an unquestionable fact that this religious group is not distinguished in general by its extreme purity of life and still less for that frame of mind which God's word sets out for us as one of the surest tests of our experiencing the living power of Christianity. On the contrary, Unitarianism seems to be resorted to not merely by those who have an aversion to Christianity but by those who are seeking to escape from the strictness of its practice, and also the obligation imposed on its adherents to be different rather than fall in with the declining manners of a dissipated age.

Unitarianism, when it comes from the mind rather than from the heart, often results from confused ideas about the difficulties, or the impossibilities, involved in orthodox Christianity. They produce what they claim are powerful arguments against the truth of the fundamental doctrines of Christianity, and then call upon men to abandon them as positions no longer tenable. But those who are inclined to yield to this attack should remember that it has pleased God to establish the constitution of things in this way and that perplexing difficulties and plausible objections may be brought against the most established truths such as, for example, the existence of a God, and many others. In every case, therefore, it behoves us, not to reject any proposition on a partial view, because it is attended with difficulties. Rather we should compare the difficulties involved with those that go with the alternative proposition which must replace it. In short, we look carefully at every aspect of the problem.

Experience will have convinced the attentive observer that it has been through lack of referring to this right and obvious principle that the Unitarians in particular have gained most of their adherents from the Church insofar as argument has contributed to their success. If the Unitarians, or even the Deists, were considered to be the masters of the field and were in their turn attacked by arguments showing that Christianity was almost certainly true, it is most likely that they would soon be quite unable to stand their ground. In short, reasoning fairly, there is no midway between absolute scepticism and true Christianity. If we reject the latter because of its difficulties, we shall be called upon still more loudly to reject every other system which has been offered for man's acceptance. This consideration might be paid more attention with advantage than it has been by those who set out to vindicate the truth of our religion. Many who are inclined from lack of consideration to abandon the great fundamental truths of Christianity would be startled by the thought that on the same grounds that they did so, they must give up any hope of finding any rest in religion, but only in unqualified atheism.

Besides those individuals who profess to reject revelation, there are those, and an increasing number, which may be called half-unbelievers who approximate in various degrees to a state of absolute unbelief. The system, if it deserves the name, of these men is grossly irrational. Hearing many assert and many deny the truth of Christianity, and not thinking seriously enough to realise that it must be either true or false, they take up a strange sort of middle stance of qualified truth. They perceive that there must be something in it, though by no means to the extent to which it is pushed by orthodox Christians. They accept the fact of future punishment, and that they themselves cannot altogether hope to escape it. They hope it will not be as hard for them as churchmen say. And though disbelieving almost every Christian doctrine they would not consider themselves to be on the side of unbelievers or to have grounds for any great apprehension in the event of Christianity proving true.

But we should remind these men that there is not a middle way. If they can be persuaded to read their Bible and not decide to reject its authority, they will have to admit that there is no ground whatever for this vain hope of escaping with a slight amount of punishment. Nor is there guilt inconsiderable. It is criminal to trifle with a long-suffering God and to despise both His invitations and His threatenings, the offer of His Spirit of grace and the precious blood of the Redeemer. Scripture's estimate is very different. '. . . how shall we escape if we ignore such a great salvation?' (Heb. 2:3). '. . . it will be more bearable for Sodom and Gomorrah on the day of judgment' (Matt. 10:15) than for those who voluntarily shut their eyes against the light which heaven's bounty has poured out on them. These half-unbelievers are even more reprehensible than downright sceptics for remaining in such a state of careless uncertainty without trying to discover the truth or otherwise of revelation. The probability, which they admit, that it may be true, imposes on them an additional obligation to enquire further. To confirmed sceptics it must be plainly stated that nowadays there is less excuse than ever for not looking into the grounds and proofs on which the truth of Christianity rests. Never before were these proofs so plain or so readily available for man's consideration. The widespread poison of unbelief has in our day been met with more numerous and powerful antidotes. What must be the feelings of these people when they open their eyes in the spirit world and are convinced, too late, of the awful reality of their impending ruin? May God in His mercy awaken them from their desperate sleep while there is still life and time for repentance!

Section IV
Advice suggested by the state of the times to true Christians

To those who really deserve the name of Christian much has been said by the way in the course of the present work. They are most important members of the community and there never was a time when this could be affirmed more justly than at the present. Let them, for their part, ponder seriously the important position which they fill and the various duties that go with it. Intelligent accounts of foreign countries, which have been recently published, indicate that religion and the standard of morality are declining everywhere abroad even more rapidly than in our own country. At the same time, the progress of irreligion, and the decay of morals at home must alarm every considerate mind, and forebode the worst consequences, unless the growing evil can be halted. We can depend only upon true Christians to render this important service. Zeal is required in the cause of religion and only they can feel it. The charge of being peculiar will be incurred and only they will dare to encounter it. Uniformity of conduct and perseverance will be required and among no others can we find such qualities.

Let true Christians, then, with suitable earnestness strive

to recommend their faith in everything, and to silence the idle gibes of ignorant objectors. Let them vindicate boldly the cause of Christ in an age when so many who bear the name of Christians are ashamed of Him. And let them consider that the important duty of halting for a while the fall of their country devolves on them. Perhaps, too, they will perform a still greater service to society, not by interference in politics but by restoring the influence of religion and of raising the standard of morality.

Let them be active, useful and generous towards others while being moderate and self-denying in themselves. Let them be as ashamed of idleness, as they would be of sin. When Providence blesses them with affluence, let them show by their modest demeanour, and by their absence of display that, without appearing odd, they are not slaves of fashion. Rather they consider it their duty to set an example of moderation and sobriety, and to reserve for nobler and more disinterested purposes the money which others selfishly waste in ostentation, dress, carriages and horses. Let them show, in short, moderation in all worldly things as becomes those whose concerns are set on objects higher than any which this world affords, and who possess, within themselves a sufficiency of satisfaction and comfort, which the world looks for in futility and dissipation. Let them cultivate a spirit of universal goodwill, and of friendly fellowship towards all those, of whatever sect or denomination, who agree with them in the great fundamental truths of religion. Let them encourage men of real piety wherever they are found, and encourage in others every attempt to restrain the progress of vice and to revive and spread the influence of religion and virtue. Let them pray earnestly and constantly that such endeavours may be successful, and that our abused, long-suffering God will continue to grant us the privilege of true Christian belief.

Let them pray continually for their country. Who knows but that the governor of the universe, who hears the prayers of His servants, may answer their intercessions and turn away our ruin, continuing to give us the fullness of those earthly blessings which we have hitherto enjoyed in such abundant measure.

We are sure, if we believe the Scripture, that God will favour the nation to which His servants belong and that, in fact, they have often been the unknown and unhonoured instruments responsible for drawing down on their country the blessings of safety and prosperity.

I should be an example of that false shame which I have condemned in others were I not to admit boldly my firm conviction that our national difficulties must both directly and indirectly be ascribed to the decline of religion and morality. The only solid hopes for the well-being of our country depend not so much on her fleets and armies, the wisdom of her rulers, or the spirit of her people, as on the realisation that she still contains many, who, in a degenerate age, love and obey the Gospel of Christ. My humble trust is that the prayers of these may still prevail and that, for their sake, God may still favour us.

Let the Christian reader also pray for the success of this feeble effort to serve true religion. God can make the weakest effort effective and the writer will feel greatly honoured if as a result of what he has written, a single fellow-creature is wakened out of false security, or a single Christian worthy of the name, is stimulated to greater usefulness. Let the writer affirm his desire not only to discharge a duty to his country, but also to fulfil what he sees as a solemn and indispensable obligation to his friends and acquaintances. Let him also affirm the genuine concern which he feels for the welfare of his fellow-creatures and express the fervent wish that while in a large part of Europe where a false philosophy is preferred to the lessons of revelation, unbelief is widespread with all the consequences that might be expected, and unrestrained licentiousness and vice prevail in this country at least there might be a place of refuge. This might be a land of religion and piety, where the blessings of Christianity could still be enjoyed and where the Redeemer's name might still be honoured. A place where people can observe the religion of Jesus with all its blessed effects and from where, God willing, the means of religious instruction and consolation might again be extended to surrounding countries, to the world at large.